HOW TO BE HAPPY

OVERCOMING MIND PROBLEMS

C.J. Jos, M.D.

ANAPHORA LITERARY PRESS

QUANAH, TEXAS

ANAPHORA LITERARY PRESS
1108 W 3rd Street
Quanah, TX 79252
https://anaphoraliterary.com

Book design by Anna Faktorovich, Ph.D.

Printed in the United States of America, United Kingdom and in Australia on acid-free paper.

Cover: "Table for Writing Implements" (Bundai). Gold and silver maki-e on black lacquer. ca. 1500. Japan. The Metropolitan Museum of Art: Gift of Florence and Herbert Irving, 2015.

Published in 2018 by Anaphora Literary Press

How to Be Happy: Overcoming Mind Problems
C.J. Jos, M.D.—1st edition.

Library of Congress Control Number: 2018905513

Library Cataloging Information
Jos, C.J., 1943-, author.
    How to be happy : Overcoming mind problems / C.J. Jos, M.D.
    224 p. ; 9 in.
    ISBN 978-1-68114-430-6 (softcover : alk. paper)
    ISBN 978-1-68114-431-3 (hardcover : alk. paper)
    ISBN 978-1-68114-432-0 (e-book)
1. Self-Help—Mood Disorders—Depression.
2. Self-Help—Personal Growth—Happiness.
3. Medical—Psychiatry—Psychopharmacology.
BF511-593 Psychology: Affection. Feeling. Emotion.
150: Psychology

HOW TO BE HAPPY

OVERCOMING MIND PROBLEMS

C.J. Jos, M.D.

CONTENTS

This book is dedicated to the men and women who have shown the courage to overcome their Mental Problems as well as Mind Problems to attain Sustained Happiness in life.

PART I

HAPPY HEALTHY MIND

INTRODUCTION

L et me begin by describing what the *Mind Problems* are and emphasizing on the importance of overcoming them to make human life happy and healthy. These are a broad range of psychological predicaments, maladaptive in nature, sandwiched between the day-to-day life experiences and the subclinical disorders. In spite of their low clinical intensity, however, they still can affect the person's thinking, behavior and wellbeing in profoundly negative ways and have the uncanny ability to eat away happiness and bring down the structure of harmony and health.

At the beginning of my professional life, if someone told me these problems were clinically significant, I would have accused that person of elevating the mundane difficulties in life to a much higher level than needed, and by doing so trivializing the real medical disorders. However, as time passed by, I realized that there were indeed several *Mind Problems*, if left unmanaged, could fester, become worse like an infected cut that turn to gangrene and bring on personal calamities and even untimely deaths.

There are many well-documented books on the role of the mental disorders in causing unhappiness, ill-health and personal calamities, however, none of them deal with the importance of the *Mind Problems*. This book is written to fill up such a huge vacuum. For the health providers, like I was in my early days, concerned about overvaluing the life's mundane problems, I am hoping, the book become thought provoking and professionally challenging.

These *Mind Problems* are encountered by everyone at some time or other and due to their frequent occurrences, they have become the mind equivalents of physical problems such as headaches, backaches and stomach upsets. It was such a trend that led the world renowned co-founder of Menninger Clinic, William Menninger to comment, "Mental health problems do not affect three or four out of every five persons but one out of one." I coined the term *Mind Problems* to avoid the stigma associated with the word *mental*.

I have named several of them - annoying stress, miserable state,

nervous tension, swinging moods, dreadful envy, obnoxious greed, undue shyness, gloomy laziness, excessive oddness, tenuous suspicions,
indecent vanity, gross arrogance, repulsive impulsivity, troublesome lying. There are others too, and each person needs to find out what they
are afflicted with by conducting a self-examination.

In his 2012 editorial, Henry A. Nasrallah, Editor-In-Chief of Current Psychiatry described the *Mind Problems* as fringe behaviors and
wrote, "Most of these are idiosyncrasies that are outside the realm of
psychopathology—usually are significantly maladaptive and could lead
to social or vocational dysfunction." He named several more- bullying,
chauvinism, fanaticism, extortion, demagoguery, corruption, bribery,
power-seeking, malice, infidelity, mendacity, cheating, cruelty, narrow-
mindedness, ruthlessness, and deceptiveness.

Unlike the mental maladies, the *Mind Problems* can look at times
docile as a lamb and innocent as a dove, and some of them due to their
infrequent appearances can give the victims a false sense of security,
however, really be the harbingers of bigger clinical issues. The stress
and burnout encountered at work may in fact be the early stages of
major depression, such progression slowly occurring without raising
any red flags. The unexpected road rage displayed on the highway can
really be the initial sign of bipolar disorder. The onset of laziness after
losing the job can be the beginning of a depressive gloom. The unusually odd behaviors in a youngster can very well be the beginning of an
obsessive-compulsive disorder. The benign looking troublesome lying
in childhood may inch towards antisocial personality disorder, loaded
with more serious troubles.

As with the mental disorders, many with their *Mind Problems* too,
indulge in wrong coping methods: a social drinker drinking even more
to relax or drugging to get high, a smoker smoking much more to calm
down the nerves, an unhappy person eating more seeking comfort and
gaining weight, and those with restless minds approaching their physicians for nerve pills or sleeping pills to shut it down. These strategies
are harmful on their own and also make the initial problems worse.
They can also distort the naturally developing clinical enhancement of
the *Mind Problems,* and delay getting the proper diagnosis.

The *Mind Problems* can take a huge physical toll as well. In 2014,
American Psychological Association reported that chronic stress, the
most studied *Mind Problem* was linked to the six leading causes of
death: heart disease, cancer, lung ailments, accidents, cirrhosis of the

liver and suicide. A study published in the British Medical Journal concluded that those with high level of stress had an increased risk of death
by 67 percent, and even more surprisingly, those with low level of stress
had a 16 percent higher risk. A larger study involving three continents
showed those engaged in high-strain jobs were 22 percent more likely
to suffer stroke.

The general tendency of those afflicted with the *Mind Problems* is
to deny or downplay their significance and this may have come from
the fear, admitting to such may be judged as a sign of human weakness.
It has to be due a powerful instinctual drive embedded in everyone, not
to be perceived as a weakling in front of the others. May be it was this
subliminal force that made a child uneasy wearing glasses in front of
his friends, middle-aged person uncomfortable having a hearing aid or
even the elderly feel awkward to be seen in the public with the walking
cane.

This forceful instinctual drive is universal, even the well-educated
and smart people succumb to it, sometimes end up paying huge prices.
The stressed-out soldiers in the battlefields who have seen too much
blood and shattered bodies, the police officers working in the high-
crime precincts having witnessed deadly shootings, and even the U.S.
physicians can become its victims. Doctors, the guardians of health
and well-being of Americans are notorious for downplaying their own
Mind Problems like stress and burnout- their suicide rates are higher
than that of the general public.

The danger in downplaying the importance of *Mind Problems* leads
to homicides as well. With each school shooting in U.S, the public
assumed that the perpetrators had to be insane to carry out such atrocious acts. However, they were perplexed when the experts could not
find any mental illnesses most of the time in these monsters. The reason, what these criminals had was only a cluster of *Mind Problems*, may
be some subclinical disorders as well, and such a pathological state of
mind, plus having access to the weapons made them dangerous killers.

In spite of all these serious concerns, the mental health establishment is still struggling with the very concept of *Mind Problems*, where
to fit them in the lexicon of the mental disorders. This hesitancy to
incorporate the new ideas and make the necessary changes in a timely
manner is very much akin to the conservative Catholic Church's reluctance to deviate from its long-held traditional values and teachings.
The powerful hindrance in case of mental health progress was the psy-

choanalytical dogmas, influencing many intellectuals, and it did not diminish even after its master, Sigmund Freud passed away. For the profession deeply entrenched in the concept of *Self,* that provided each person the sense of being separate and distinct from others, and created the self-awareness of '*who I am,*' it was not be easy to accept the *Mind Problems* as significant, since they were very much glued to the day-to-day life experiences.

Ironically, the psychiatric establishment had been through this road before, however, handled it successfully. In late 1970s, the worshippers of *birth trauma* and *psychic trauma* with their constant attempt to elevate the internal stress at the expense of obvious, external stresses were overtaken by the tsunami tidal waves brought on by the gruesome Vietnam War. Their biological colleagues were able to see clearly through the muddy waters, both the psychic as well as physical symptoms due to directly experiencing the traumatic event. Post-*Traumatic Stress* Disorder—PTSD made its debut into the Diagnosis-Hall of Fame in 1980.

Biological Empire

My professional life began studying the intricacies of human body, including that of the brain; however, it slowly channeled to the less-defined waters of the human mind. During this decades-long eventful journey, I witnessed the rapid decline of the psychoanalytical world built up by Sigmund Freud, the powerful emergence of biological empire put together by the neuropsychiatrists, and the crowning of brain as its emperor and the mind as the mysterious queen. In the calm post-Second World War climate, the pragmatic brain scientists figured out that the supreme highway to the queen's castle was laid through the brain's hills and valleys and the hidden treasures tucked inside. Excited, they brought forth novel biochemical theories and an array of medications that confirmed their suspicions. The well-nourished stallion, the biological psychiatry of neurons, synapses and neurotransmitters galloped on, overcoming the fences and ditches in its way. The highly caricatured zombie-look appearance brought on by the new drugs or the anti-psychiatry movement energized by Thomas Szasz or the release of a captivating movie titled, *One Flew over the Cuckoo's Nest* were not enough to slow down its steady pace.

No doubt at all, the biological psychiatry enriched by the rational brain science is here to stay, since its foundation is healthy. The pharmaceutical companies just happened to be at the right place at the right time, to use their skills to the maximum and reap the rewards. There were thousands of scientists behind this show, and millions of patients benefitted from this heartening adventure. I am hopeful of a brighter future for biological psychiatry that will take a closer look into the significant *Mind Problems* as well, and come up with effective scientific remedies.

At this juncture, let me make it very clear, I am not advocating the *Mind Problems* to be elevated to the status of the clinical disorders. Absolutely not. What I am suggesting, the psychiatry establishment has to pay closer attention to these psychological predicaments in causing mental havocs and human tragedies, and encourage its practitioners to look into their impact on the mental illnesses and assess them for possible treatments.

Management

The professional pariah attitude towards *Mind Problems* extends even to their management, creating a double standard—It is alright to take couple of Tylenol for headache, even though headache is only a symptom and not an illness. How about getting assessed for the medication treatment to deal with stress and burnout, arrogance and volatility? No way; no pill treatment for these problems. They do not even come close to the clinical dais, and only such disorders have such privilege! Millions of people with subclinical disorders and significant *Mind Problems* have been denied due treatment from this erroneous attitude. I am hoping this book will be an eye opener for those who still carry on with this double standard.

A piece of good news; already many psychologists and some psychiatrists are managing the *Mind Problems*, not getting paid a dime from the insurance companies, since the victims lack a *real* diagnosis, encrypted in the American Psychiatric Association's Diagnostic and Statistical Manual (DSM). The youngsters in this predicament are good candidates to enforce a clinical strategy, employ preemptive strike. In this population, the substance abuse problems often begin with an occasional beer or smoking marijuana, the conduct disorder may emerge as an isolated incident of cruelty to the pet or repeated lying, and even a bipolar disorder can show up early with only impulsive actions, especially in a family loaded with such history. The vigilant parents should seek out psychotherapy to prevent a behavior problem growing to a full-size clinical disorder.

Stress and burnout, miserable mind states and nervousness, swinging moods and suspicions, repulsive impulsivity and gross arrogance are some of the better candidates to be evaluated for the medication treatment. Some *Mind Problems* may indeed be camouflaging more significant problems- shyness can be a notch below the social anxiety disorder; laziness of recent onset very well can be a low grade depression; arrogance, impulsivity and greed can be part of a subclinical bipolar disorder; envy and odd behaviors can be part of a shadow-OCD.

As I unambiguously stated before, the Mind Problems in Italics were not mental disorders and should not be subjected to medication treatment straightway. In fact, the meds should never be the first line in their management, especially in the youngsters. Even for the adults, initially they should try to correct their problems on their own. Many can succeed depending on their educational competence, psychological sophistication and internet awareness and if the problem not contaminated with the substance abuse. If the self-employed strategies failed, the professional help should be sought.

The main thrust of this book is to encourage each person to build up their own house of happiness to make life on earth purposeful and meaningful. This is well-achievable goal if the foundation of this house healthy, devoid of any mental disorders and *Mind Problems*. Overcoming the mental disorders will always need profession help; the *Mind Problems* may need such help if the self-employed strategies are not working. Hopefully, the mental health establishment will come forward to accept the *Mind Problems* too as significant and if so, it is likely to encourage the practitioners to consider them in their clinical management.

CHAPTER 1
HORROR ON THE
BRIDGE

I began to think about the factors that contributed to happiness and the barriers to achieving it, after I had a humiliating panic attack for no apparent reason, on a seemingly never-ending bridge in Louisiana. What happened was so unexpected and puzzling, it got me to deliberate over the *Mind Problems* that did not reach the mental disorder status, since that's what I had. According to the American Psychiatric Association's Manual, only recurrent panic attacks deserve the diagnosis of Panic Disorder. However, I found out even one panic attack had the punching power to erode my inner happiness.

Before going any further, let me introduce you to the Louisiana trip that led me to assess my problem, novel to me. Even with my long professional life as a psychiatrist, I had never experienced anything like this before. I took my personal experience seriously with no desire to minimize its importance or dismiss it as a trivial onetime event.

Humiliation

It happened on the 23-mile-long Lake Pontchartrain Causeway Bridge near New Orleans, several years before Hurricane Katrina breached nearly every levee of this metropolis and killed or displaced thousands on its path, the destruction so huge that the name *Katrina* was officially retired by the World Meteorological Organization.

Driving from St. Louis, Missouri, we got close to our destination late in the evening, well after sunset. My wife and two children were with me and I was looking forward to the stay in the city that had become famous for its cuisine, music, Mardi Gras festivities, French Quarter and Bourbon Street. In spite of the thick darkness, as we neared the metropolis I felt like we were driving over a bridge that stretched forever. Mile after mile as I stared ahead in the darkness, I saw an endless white line ahead, guiding me forward, occasionally punctuated by bright light from the headlights of cars coming from the opposite direction. At the time, the feelings were not strong enough to whip up any emotions, just felt a dull sense of apprehension inside.

However, everything changed on our return trip under bright sunlight. As soon as we entered the bridge, I experienced an uneasy feeling building up, my chest pushing forward as if it were ready to explode. My imagination began to run wild with dreadful thoughts of all the things that could happen. A multitude of scenarios flooded my mind, one disaster after another exploding in my brain. My heart was pumping more furiously than ever, my breathing becoming faster, my throat choking up, my mouth was quickly drying out, my eyes fogged over and my palms became drenched with sweat. I became terrified that the steering wheel might slip out of my wet hands.

Frantically I wanted to stop, but only saw small side-pockets along the side of the bridge, perhaps one every half mile. I glanced helplessly as I sped by the small spaces since I believed they were too short to stop the car and hand over the wheel to my wife. I found myself fearing that if I attempted to stop the vehicle, I would not be able to and the concrete walls would not withstand the crash and crumble, and the car plunge to the deep waters below. I pictured a scenario where my foot would be on the accelerator rather than the brake. Somehow, I continued to drive imagining the worst, looking outside calm and in control, but inside there was a raging ocean of fear that everything would soon come to a crashing end.

Meanwhile, my wife who was sitting beside me and my kids in the back seat had no idea what I was experiencing. Instead, they were enjoying the wide variety of gulls, ducks, geese, and sparrows flying around in flocks, occasionally snatching a fish and warily looking out for the crocodiles that sometimes popped their heads up out of the water. No one noticed the internal explosion I was experiencing. Only after we crossed the bridge, I dared to tell them what just happened. They laughed it off and joked about my nervous revelation. "Oh, it's not a big deal," my daughter said. In her teenage years, she was too young to comprehend what I went through. My wife was simply amused.

I felt humiliated and less of a man in front of my own family. Unlike many people with their first panic attack who would suspect a heart event or some catastrophic emergency, I did not think about those possibilities. My heart was thudding against the chest but I was absolutely certain what I had was only due to anxiety; nothing more than that.

I had to determine if my experience was a single, unusual, unexpected reaction due to being on a long drive or if it was more complicated. I questioned my reaction thinking perhaps my thoughts went into overdrive and triggered emotional fears, so maybe this was a simple aberration. Immediately, my brain began sending questions, such as, "What if this is not a single episode?" "What if this is the beginning of a new chapter in my life?" With my brain sending out the first salvo the ideas and questions began bombarding my mind. Would the bombardment of queries going to destroy me? Was this like the microbes getting inside the human body after breaking through the solid defense of the immune system and once in, continuing to play havoc with its targets? Or, maybe it was more like a wolf pack trailing a herd of elk or caribou, looking for an animal that displayed any sign of weakness. Was it possible that the brain registered my weakness on the initial journey through the bridge and waited until the return trip to blast me to pieces?

Would being the victim of one attack make me susceptible to future ones? Having learned how to humiliate me by penetrating my psychic armor, it could try again on perhaps a shorter bridge such as the JB Bridge over the Mississippi River which is close to my home. Even worse, what if this happened in front of the medical students or my patients? I did not want to take a chance and decided then and there that I have to play solid offense now, to prevent any future calamities.

Mending with the Pill

I considered different options to correct my problem. There were therapies of the mind available or I could practice yoga or meditation, or get into a vigorous exercise program to relax my body and mind. However, since I was more tuned to the principles of brain biology than psychology of the mind in my own practice and teaching, I was already predisposed to use the biological sciences to explain and treat the *Mind Problems*. Moreover, I had witnessed the tremendous transformations in my patients due to medications, so I was eager to try it in my own case. I did not think it necessary to consult another doctor, since I believed he would simply agree with me that I had a panic attack with no physiological causes to explain it. Further, I believed he would say, since I had only one attack, it did not qualify as a mental disorder and that meant I was not a candidate for medication treatment.

I decided to read more on the efficacy of taking pills to manage *Mind Problems* that did not attain clinical diagnostic status. One such book I read was the 1993 book by Peter D. Kramer, *Listening to Prozac*. Kramer wondered if Prozac, the pill introduced a few years earlier, could alter a person's personality through what he called *cosmetic pharmacology*. He considered the ethical implications of giving a drug to alter the personality or help a person achieve success, such as by climbing in a career, or for that matter, to deny a person that possibility. Then, having decided it was ethical to use a drug for such a result, he concluded that Prozac gave unhappy, but not necessarily depressed people, uplift in life. Among other things, it increased their self-confidence and helped them deal with the setbacks in life without getting upset.

Prozac belonged to the group of medications called SSRIs—Selective Serotonin Reuptake Inhibitors that revolutionized the health field by helping to alleviate a wide variety of mental symptoms. The once-a-day dosage and the absence of significant side-effects made it popular. Thus, I began treatment on my own, using Celexa (citalopram), another SSRI with a shorter half-life than Prozac (fluoxetine), and patiently waited for the pill to kick in.

Science Behind it

My personal experience with the medication reaffirmed my faith in the biology of the brain and its superior influence on the psychology of mind. However, it was not as simple as that. I was well-aware of the mind part of the human brain that made us who we were and defined our unique thoughts, feelings, passions and fantasies. The surprise was, in return they had the distinct ability to change the chemistry of the brain itself, a phenomenon the scientists call *neuroplasticity*. The environment around us also had this unique ability to alter the neuronal landscape of brain cells and brain connections, affecting what emerged out of it. Wow, what a revelation!

A series of discoveries beginning in 1935 brought forth serotonin, a powerful nerve transmitter which played a major role in generating a sense of well-being, while too little of it caused depression and anxiety. Then in 1987, medications like Prozac arrived on the clinical scene. Prozac increased serotonin in those who did not have enough of it in their brains. This major breakthrough marked an exciting new chapter in the history of psychiatry.

According to Barry Jacobs, the Princeton neuroscientist, depression occurred when the growth of new brain cells were suppressed. In his view, the stress was the most important factor impeding their growth, while medications like Prozac and Celexa boosted the serotonin levels that kicked off the production of new brain cells, which allowed the depression to lift. As simple as that! It meant the clinical depression had a close affinity with stress, a *Mind Problem* experienced by most people at some time or other. However, many would consider their *Mind Problems* as a part of normal day-to-day living, minimizing their importance. Yet, as shown by scientific research using twin and family studies, these problems if moderately severe and lasted long enough, deregulated the biological rhythms and had the ability to cause significant damage to health and wellbeing.

Transformation

I knew the chemical molecules in the pill would have to travel to the serotonin reserves inside my brain to boost the level up, since too low a level contributed to depressions as well as panic attacks. I hoped they would reach there in the right amount to be effective, not in excess to produce any ill effects. I prayed none of it would get into the serotonin reserves in the gastrointestinal tract causing side-effects.

I compared the process to Neil Armstrong's trip to the moon in 1969, the journey of about 240,000 miles from earth, taking some days to get there. The whole world was exhilarated upon hearing the news and in my heightened state of awareness after the panic attack, I felt almost the same way, waiting for the chemical to reach its intended destination. It took about three weeks for this to happen, even though the travel distance was miniscule! Nonetheless, I felt the effect as soon as it touched upon the intended destination in the desired amount. But unlike the voices and pictures that came to the people on earth from the moon, what I experienced was a new set of feelings and ideas. I felt much happier, my self-confidence soared to a higher level, and I had an urge to walk with my body straighter than before, chin held high. I was not certain if others noticed the change, since nobody commented about it, but the change was very real for me.

Other changes occurred over the next several weeks. My personal habits and views altered. At one time, I loved country music, but now my fascination with it diminished and I often forgot to turn on the radio while going to sleep. I also became more conservative in my social views. Rooting for the underdog was a universal phenomenon, and from early on in my life, I always sided with the little guy, yelling louder and clapping harder when he won the fight. I had no sympathy for Goliath, the pagan giant brought down by young David. I supported the victims of racism, such as the black seamstress Rosa Parks against the white bus driver, Nelson Mandela against apartheid in South Africa and Martin Luther King against the vast racial discrimination prevalent in the United States. I felt a special sympathy for African-Americans, whom I thought of as the underdogs of an amazing American civilization.

The pill changed these attitudes and more. I no longer felt the same pull to defend and support the underdog. When I heard the oft-cited statement that more young black men were in prison than in college, or read about the deprived childhoods or ravages of slavery, I no longer felt the call to rise up to defend these victims. Likewise, my views on capital punishment changed too. I was strongly opposed to it, but now I could rationalize it for vicious crimes, since it provided closure to the grieving family. I revised my attitude toward abortion as well, which I had considered as an issue to be worked out between the woman and her doctor. But now, for the first time, I wondered if there were too many abortions across the world and could see adoption as an alternative. As a practicing Catholic, I also felt less bothered by the existence of dysfunctional priests inside the Church, since I now viewed religion as something between God and me.

Even my political views transformed. At one time, I was a staunch Democrat, but now I realized I was becoming a lightweight Republican. I even voted for a Republican candidate for the first time, convincing myself that it was the people that mattered, not the party slogans.

I accepted there were good hearted people in both parties. Instead of viewing all the Republicans as rich people who cared only about Wall Street, I recognized that many of them cared for the people on Main Street as well.

Meanwhile, as I experienced these changes in my thinking, I received recognition for being a good teacher and employee. After being in the health field for over 20 years, teaching the medical students and residents at St. Louis University, I received a teacher of the year award for the first time. Around the same time, the Missouri State Department of Mental Health selected me as the best employee of the month. Both awards came as happy surprises!

By this time, the Louisiana Bridge was becoming a distant memory, no longer able to whip up any emotions. I could think of crossing any bridge, whenever I wanted, without any concern over my heart pumping too fast, or my throat getting choked up, or my mouth becoming dry. I had no uneasy feeling crossing the mighty Mississippi River while traveling from Missouri to Illinois. I knew my rewarding experience with the pill, though not unique, was not that common. Most people felt a gradual elevation in their mood and a decrease in anxiety after taking it for two to three weeks. Rarely, some bipolar depressed patients became too happy with it.

Analyzing the Experience

Going through these changes, I asked myself if all of these experiences happened due to this pill, or could at least some of them may have been pure coincidences that occurred around the same time. I eventually concluded that the changes in the first several weeks and months definitely were due to the pill. Though I was less certain about the events that took longer to happen, I felt the pill may have played a part in my renewed enthusiasm and self-confidence. Moreover, I rationalized that some of the changes were justified, since my views on African-Americans were more well-balanced now, and I had a more mature outlook on abortion, taking arguments from both sides into consideration.

I also wondered if these highly positive feelings generated by the pill could be due to a mood problem lying dormant, now coming out wearing the happiness uniform. However, I did not care as long as the changes I experienced were reasonable and I could explain them to myself without trepidation. With the new boldness within me, my top priority now was to live a happy life, with less concern about the trivialities of today and the ambiguities of tomorrow.

Concept of Self

I always liked who I was with my own assets and liabilities, proud to be that unique person, knowing no one else born in the same way. So, after all this being said and done, I took a deeper look inside of myself to find out if I lost *any of me* in this process. Initially, no clear answers came to me. However, there were other questions popped up in my mind. If a chemical molecule had the ability to change the thoughts and feelings, beliefs and habits, was it evidence for us not having as much control over ourselves as we assumed to be the case? Were we simply at the mere mercy of the nerve connections and neurochemicals inside the brain? Did these hard wiring and chemical soups have the power to shake up our inner self? Did this mean our emotional responses, such as happiness on a joyous occasion, sadness upon the loss of a loved one, or anger aroused in support a justifiable cause, were not really spontaneous? Did these normal emotional responses emerge from within us, without our full acknowledgement and acceptance?

Self is the well-accepted, long-cherished concept defining who we are, outwardly showing only a tiny fraction of it. Long before the modern neuroscience emerged, Freud asserted that much of our *Self* emerged from our unconscious, without our full permission. Maybe this psychic part hiding deep inside the brain was the neuronal synapses and neurotransmitters that got ignited without our full control. It is not easy to admit such lack of control, since it would mean abdicating our controlling identity of who we are. Acknowledging that the powerful man, the master of universe not in charge of himself and was at the mercy of brain's chemical changes would crack up the very foundations of who we had been, challenging the cherished dogmas firmly held by humanity for a long time.

However, after analyzing further the changes experienced by the pill, I reached the conclusion that my *Self* as described by Carl Rogers had not changed at all. My inner core personality was exactly the same and was untouched by any chemical. "The most basic part of the self-scheme or self-concept; the sense of being separate and distinct from others and the awareness of the constancy of the self" as explained by Bee, H.L. in 1992 in *The Developing Child* was in my full control. What the medication did was allow me to change certain things in my life with my approval. In the big picture of human personality, the extent of these changes was miniscule, less than a tiny piece of limestone of huge Empire State Building.

Regrets

I did not want to dismiss what happened to me as a random occurrence in life, like a one-in-a-million chance to win the jackpot. Definitely, it was not. In fact, my blissful experience made me look at the common *Mind Problems* in a different light, seeing diverse colors dispersed through the newly discovered prism. It also made me to take a deeper look into my past, in search of any mistakes I may have made in ignoring their significance.

The most unfortunate one happened with my father. He was 80 years old when I spent time with him while I was on a trip to India. While watching television together, he causally told me that he felt tired all the time. The bright son's mind instantly went into action! Was he anemic? What about his thyroid status? My first question was if he had blood work done recently. He said yes and all results were normal. Case closed! It was much later that I realized what he had a low grade depression and I did a big disservice to him in not advising him to take an antidepressant to correct his tired feeling.

I am not sure if my father knew if he was depressed or not. Maybe, he did not want to feel disgraced by telling me so. However, I have often come across patients in my practice who were not certain if they physically or mentally tired. Subjectively, it should not be that difficult to separate the two, but many did not take the time and effort to distinguish between these conditions. With practice, it should be as easy as knowing the temperature inside the house without looking at the thermostat!

I also became more sensitive to the minor clinical problems of my patients. If a person complained of being tired, stressed or burnt out, I was now willing to bring these problems into clinical consideration, instead of arbitrarily dismissing them as life experiences. Some of them I referred for psychotherapy, while I prescribed medications for others. If I waited for these people to meet the clinical diagnostic criteria, I would be denying them the relief they deserved. It was highly possible that some of them could have perished in the midst of their chaos.

CHAPTER 2
HEALTHY MIND

The human brain is the most complex *machine* that has ever existed, making human beings the master of the universe and well-beyond, capable of touching the moon and playing around with the stars. This jelly-like mass of about three pounds tucked inside the safety of the skull is the supreme commander from the time each life begins, to be continued until the very end. Scientists have chartered every nook and corner of the human body and measured the performance of all body parts, however, continue to be mystified by this last human frontier of hills and valleys, wired with some billions neurons and trillions of synapses.

Homo sapiens emerged about 400,000 years ago on the surface of planet earth, with their brains becoming larger and grander than their predecessors. This vastly complex structure kept on improving, giving up the hammer stones and hand axes of times past and learning to make new gadgets for survival and pleasure—'Barbs were connected to the fishing sticks, knives made sharper and longer, and sewing needles fashioned thinner and finer.' This progress continued in astonishing ways to the modern times, by developing supercomputers and artificial intelligence machines, even reaching an extraterrestrial land—the moon.

Brain Development

The master organ begins to form from the 16th day of conception, as a neural plate, consisting of a platform of nerve cells. Over the next few days, a trench is formed in the plate, called the neural groove. When its edges meet by the 21st day, a neural tube forms, and its front part becomes the brain itself, while the rest of it develops into the spinal cord. As simple as that!

The developmental process is driven by a person's genetic code, which affects exactly how the brain is configured of neurons and synapses, much like how the director of an action-packed movie may decide how its many parts, from actors' actions to their dialogue, come together to form the whole movie. The hard-wired, preprogrammed brain is set up to respond reflexively from the beginning. The newborn brain continues to add neuronal cells and connections over the first few years of life, growing at an amazing pace. It doubles in size in the first year alone and by age three reaches 80 percent of its adult volume, ready to suck in the experiences of a life time.

Mind Location

Early man should have known the soft tissue-mass held inside the head-bone was very special, having noticed the profound mind changes brought on by its injuries from wild beasts and untamed nature. However, surprisingly, Aristotle, the student of Plato and teacher of Alexander the Great, considered the heart as the organ of thinking, perception and feelings, whereas the brain was important to keep the body's temperature. Roman physician Galen the Great who came to the scene later on, rejected those ideas, however, paid more attention to the brain coverings and cavities than to the brain itself. In the sixteenth century, Andreas Vesalius who was referred to as the founder of modern human anatomy rejected the theory of ventricular localization of mental skills, however, even he continued to give credence to those brain cavities as a place for storage of *animal spirits*, from where they would depart following the nerves, to reach the muscles or the sense organs. In the following century, Rene Descartes, the French philosopher and scientist considered pineal body as the center of mind activity. The belief that animal spirits travelled along the nerves continued, until the electric nature of nerve conduction was finally verified in the eighteenth century.

The neurologist turned psychoanalyst Sigmund Freud born in 1856 dominated the mind empire and his mind theories became highly popular from early twentieth century. He popularized the topographical model of mind and used the metaphor of an iceberg to explain it. For him, only a small amount of the iceberg was above the surface, representing the conscious mind, where all the mental processes of which we were aware of took place—The preconscious mind was just below the surface and contained the thoughts and feelings that a person not aware of, but which could easily be brought to consciousness—The huge mass below the surface was the unconscious mind, inaccessible to consciousness but influenced judgments, feelings and behavior tremendously. In 1923 Freud came up with another of his master-piece, the architectural model of mind, describing id, ego and superego as its pivotal parts.

Today, the modern neuro-psychiatry has no difficulty in accepting the mind emerging from several brain parts. In this era dominated by computer sciences, many of their experts will agree with David Rudrauf at the University of Iowa in Iowa City, who said that mental functions might not be tied to fixed brain regions—Instead, the mind might be more like a virtual machine running on distributed computers, with brain resources allocated in a flexible manner. The bottom line is the Brain and Mind are like conjoint twins and one cannot function without the other. Any brain injury not only imbalances the human body, but also clouds the precious mind, the supreme commander in charge of our thoughts and feelings, desires and fantasies. Likewise, any harm occurred to the mind affects the harmonious flow of all body functions, including that of brain.

Body vs. Mind

I wrote the following Hindu story to illustrate this close, unbreakable connection of body and mind. Lord Shiva and wife Parvati were in deep, peaceful meditation at the summit of legendary Mount Kailash, when a group of wise men and women arrived from the holy city of Rameswaram and woke them up.

"We are seeking an answer to a vexing question," said one of the wise men. "Which is more powerful, body or mind?"

"The body," Shiva answered promptly. "The body has the brain in it, and the brain has the mind inside it so the body is definitely more powerful."

The wise men were excited by what they heard. "That is what we thought, Lord," said one wise man.

But the wise women whispered among themselves, because they did not agree. "We think it is the mind that is more powerful," one of them said.

Parvati quickly agreed with them. "The mind is definitely more powerful, because even a physically crippled person can be happy, if the mind is healthy. However, even a physically healthy person with a crippled mind will not find happiness."

Shiva was surprised by her answer, since his wife usually agreed with him. So now he felt the question should be decided independently. He addressed the group, "Since my wife and I are of two different opinions, let us see what the ordinary people think, so we can come to some agreement. Therefore, I will send two of you, a man with only a body but no mind, and a woman with only a mind, but no body to spend time with common folks, to find out the right answer."

Two volunteers came forward, and for the next few weeks they visited the people in many villages. When they returned, they each recounted their story. The wise man told his story first. "I was the one with only a body, but no mind. When I reached the Himalayan valleys, I rolled down the fluffy snow to generate pleasure. However, I experienced no pleasure since I did not have a mind. Next I went to River Ganges and took a holy dip, but I did not feel the water or smell the aroma from burning herbs. Then, I headed to a desert where I came across a beautiful Rajput princess taking a camel ride by herself. However, I did not have any feelings for her, since I had no mind. So, I continued mindlessly on my journey, just walking, but seeing and feeling nothing."

Then, the wise woman told her story. "I was the woman with only a mind, but no body. Reaching my hometown, I was shocked to find out that my only child had died in an accident. I felt very sad and cried loudly, but nobody heard my crying, because I did not have a voice. No tears came down, because I had no eyes. Then, I wanted to give the last purification bath to my child as was the custom in the village; but I could not, because I had no hands. Later, after my child's cremation, I wanted to eat ghee rice prepared by family and friends to comfort the deceased soul, but I could not eat anything because I had no mouth."

After hearing both stories, Lord Shiva responded. "Thank you both for telling your stories. Now I can see that both body and mind are equally powerful. Everyone needs both, the physical body to act and the mind to think and feel. So that is the answer. The body and mind

form two parts of the whole." The wise men and women were satisfied, recognizing that body and mind depended on each other and one
could not live without the other.

Dear reader, do you agree with Lord Shiva—Both body and mind
was equally powerful. Answers would be even more varied, if comparing the healthy body with healthy mind. What if the body was healthy
and mind diseased? What if the body was crippled, however, the mind
healthy? There would not be any easy answers. For many concerned
about becoming old, it was all about their loss of independence brought
on by physical problems and memory impairment.

Mind Development

When the brain development began, it initially did not contain
a mind inside. But at some point, the mind begins to emerge inside
the brain folds, though scientists do not agree on when exactly this
happens. Did it begin functioning inside the rapidly developing brain
when it registered sense of touch by the 8th week of pregnancy, taste
by 12th week, or when it could hear sounds at 22 to 24 weeks? Or was
the mind totally blank at birth, in keeping with the *tabula rasa* theory
of John Locke, who believed that the babies were born without built-
in mental content, like a blank sheet of paper with nothing written on
it.

Modern research has totally rejected Locke's theory and strongly
favors the concept that the mind developed well before birth, filled
in with sensations and perceptions as the brain grew. The birth brings
the child to totally new experiences, described by psychoanalyst Nor-
man Cameron, "birth expels the child from the warm, dark monotony
of the uterine waters, into a world of everlasting change and infinite
space." With instinctual automatic responses, an infant that experiences pain reacts by crying and pulling away from whatever caused it,
and acting on the pleasure principle will instinctively begin sucking on
mother's breast to get the milk for immediate gratification. Soon the
child shows his or her own character traits with a propensity to behave
in certain ways.

Today, we take the intimate relationship between the brain and the
mind for granted. The conjoint twins need each other to live and thrive

on. The elegant mind defines who we are and brings out our rational and mysterious thoughts, passions, feeling and fantasies. They, as well as our behaviors and environmental input have the unique ability to rewire the brain and change the landscape through neuroplasticity.

Control over the Mind

Parents and loved ones are in control of the newborn child from the very beginning, protecting from any harm, providing enough nourishment and guiding through a healthy life style. The little ones who already have own mind, with predetermined personality traits and raw emotions, develops new skills as days and weeks pass by. Through the years the child grows up showing own whims and fancies, additionally influenced by the teachers and peers. The teenage years are notably a testing period for parents, when the youngster starts shaping their identity in new ways. However, most kids slowly learn to modulate their desires within the rules and regulations of family and society at large.

This importance of *control* was emphasized by Dag Hammarskjold, who was Secretary-General of the United Nations from 1953 until his death in a plane crash in 1961. As he stated, "We are not permitted to choose the frame of our destiny. But what we put into it is ours." The frame of destiny in which we have no choice consists of our gender, race, time and place of birth, culture born into, our parents, siblings, and other givens bestowed on us and defined who we are. Most people would try to make out the best out of these so-called *no choices*—maintaining good relationship with family members, enjoying the richness of the culture born into, and even making a move if not happy with the place of birth. Those with healthy minds are likely to succeed in these ventures.

Choices in Life

Beyond the frame of destiny, what we put into it is ours. These choices would define us substantially, good ones paving the way to sustained happiness, bad ones making life miserable and unhappy. As Wayne Dyer, the author and motivational speaker pointed out, "Our lives are a sum total of the choices we have made." In other words, we create our own destiny, again and again by selecting from the choices, and those who make the best ones getting its rich rewards.

Making life choices may not be deliberate all the time, some falling into an unhealthy pattern brought on by their willful acts and unfortunate life events. Those who are lucky keep on making positive choices with their healthy and happy genes and upbringing, based on a solid value system. However, even they need to watch out for any downward spirals; examples can be someone who made an excellent educational choice, but then got distracted and flunked out or someone who started out in a professional career with much excitement, but later lost pleasure in doing their work, or a marriage born out of romanticism and glamour lost its luster and vibrancy. In such disturbing situations, one should search for the answers internally to find out if the mind contaminated by mental disorders or even significant mind problems.

Conclusion

At birth, each one of us has been provided with a brain that looks the same in everyone; however, with a mind of its own, thinking and behaving differently one person to other. We begin living with what is granted to us, enhancing it with a vast array of tools provided and have the potential to expand it a million times more than inherited at the beginning, if we keep it healthy and without injury. However, attaining happiness in life and making the daily living meaningful is more than having a healthy mind. It is impossible to build our house of happiness, if its foundation cracked open by mental disorders and even significant *Mind Problems*. Only a healthy mind will help each person to make good choices in life, and such choices will nourish the mind even more to keep it healthy and happy.

CHAPTER 3
HAPPY MIND

Happiness is a powerful and positive emotion, adding color, excitement, and energy to daily human existence and providing a deeper meaning and contentment to the human soul. Life without it becomes like a drab, dreary, black-and-white, slow-motion movie with a broken reel. By contrast, happiness would be the vision of Julie Andrews erupting like a golden fountain on the beautiful Salzburg hills in Austria, in the movie *Sound of Music*, her utterly perfect pitch exploding with optimistic, cheerful lyrics, "Raindrops on roses and whiskers on kittens, bright copper kettles and warm woolen mittens... Cream colored ponies and crisp apple strudels..."

The instinctual desire to be happy is embedded in all of us and can be achieved by anyone with a healthy mental foundation, devoid of mental disorders and significant *Mind Problems*. We often come across stories of the well-known people whose edifice of happiness collapsed due to their shaky foundation, money or fame unable to sustain it. Marilyn Monroe was dealt a cruel hand from the very beginning of her life and did not succeed in spite of her *glamour* and beauty. At the other end of spectrum was Elvis Presley, who had a healthy mental foundation to begin with, however, he too collapsed under the weight of massive amounts of prescription drugs he consumed.

I deliberately included this chapter *Happy Mind* to emphasize on the importance of happiness in our daily lives and the impossibility of achieving this state of mind, if the mind contaminated with mental disorders and significant *Mind Problems*. Monroe struggled all her life to find her share of happiness; however, did not succeed due to segments of mental illness she inherited. Presley lost it due to utter carelessness with what began as a *Mind Problem*. He sought instant relief and pleasure through the pills, which turned into a misadventure of vast proportions. Happiness remained elusive towards the end of his life.

At other end of the spectrum, we read the stories of those who ascended to the top through sheer guts and excellent strategies, and in that process made the world a better place to live. We hardly ever think about their mental health, knowing full well there was no way they could have reached those heights without happy healthy minds. I created the narratives of three famous men to emphasize this point: Mahatma Gandhi, John F. Kennedy, and Martin Luther King, Jr.

Mahatma Gandhi

It was a chilly morning in New Delhi on January 30, 1948. No uniformed guards stood at the entrance to Birla House where Gandhi stayed. Its large all-purpose room was fully carpeted. At one end, a wooden table was piled with correspondence, and next to it was Gandhi's famous charkha, the wheel that created *energy*.

At other end of the room, Mahatma, then 78, sat on a thick cotton mattress, reclining on a huge pillow. Soon after he finished praying and opened his eyes, his assistant Manu brought him a glass of hot water mixed with a tablespoonful of honey and lime. Once Gandhi finished it, I imagine myself asking him this question: "Mr. Gandhi, are you happy?"

He would have answered, "Yes, by grace of God."

Even the social upheavals going on all around him didn't faze him, since he still had his overriding sense of purpose, which gave him a feeling of assurance that he was on the right path and gave him peace. Thus, when I ask him, "How do you feel about the communal riots and atrocious killings happening all around you?" he would reply, "By grace of God, they will get better."

He was highly optimistic. Despite the turmoil in the world around him, Gandhi felt a deep contentment with his life and actions that were a source of happiness for him. Thus, when a delegation of Hindus and Muslims arrived to discuss with him the ways to stop the riots, Gandhi welcomed them with a smiling face. He had no idea he would be killed due to the turmoil that evening, but he felt deep happiness until the end.

John F. Kennedy

On November 22, 1963, as a light rain fell in Fort Worth, Texas, thousands of people had gathered outside the hotel where the Kennedys had spent the night. When the handsome 46-year-old President came out smiling to address them, he was met with thunderous applause.

Then, he told them, "There are no faint hearts in Fort Worth. I appreciate your being here this morning. Mrs. Kennedy will join us shortly."

After saying a few more words, Kennedy reached out to shake hands with the admiring Texans, and I imagine myself asking him, "Mr. President, are you happy?"

"Yes, I am," he would have answered, pointing to the adoring crowd below, "Look at all these happy, smiling faces. They all are waiting to vote for me next year."

So, like Gandhi, Kennedy felt a sense of fulfilment at having reached the pinnacle of his success, and he could feel that accomplishment in the admiration of the cheering crowd, which made him happy, though he had no idea what would happen to him later that day in Dallas.

Martin Luther King, Jr.

That fateful day on April 4, 1968 was supposed to be just another day along the way for Martin Luther King, Jr. to bring his vision to the people. He was in Tennessee to support the sanitation workers' strike. The day before, he had spoken at the Bishop Charles Mason Temple, knowing there were threats against his life. Be that as it may, he told the pastors and the people there, "I don't know what will happen now. We've got some difficult days ahead. But it really doesn't matter to me now, because I've been to the mountaintop... I want you to know tonight, that we, as a people, will get to the Promised Land... I'm not worried about anything. I'm not fearing any man. Mine eyes have seen the glory of the coming of the Lord."

So did he feel happy? I imagine myself asking him that question: "Mr. King, are you happy?"

He would have answered without hesitation: "Yes, I am. I just wanted to do God's will. And He's allowed me to go up to the mountaintop. And I've looked over and I've seen the Promised Land. So yes, I am a happy man."

The next day, standing on the balcony in Memphis, the man who had given his mesmerizing "I Have a Dream" speech and who was acknowledged worldwide as a hero, had no idea of the doom that would soon befall him. Yet before that fateful end, he had achieved happiness through having his dream as inspired by his faith that guided him each day.

King, President, or great spiritual leader, it did not matter unless this person was happy deep inside. Only such a powerful and positive emotion could provide the excitement and energy they needed to accomplish the tasks ahead and define their lives in such meaningful ways. The tools each of them used were different, but they could not have achieved their goals unless they were happy in their lives and also with what they did. If any had tried to build facades and smokescreens, those would vanish even by gentle winds of reality. By all accounts, Gandhi, Kennedy, and King had healthy and happy mental dispositions, enabling them to pursue their dreams, and each found their fulfillment by helping others to achieve their own dreams.

Other Pathways

There were several others, who not satisfied with what life offered, put their ideas into action by pursuing different paths to achieve happiness. Father Damien ministered to people stricken with leprosy who were placed under quarantine on the island of Moloka, and he was determined to find happiness through this unique adventure. His supreme personal sacrifice was carried out for sixteen long years, caring for the physical, spiritual, and emotional needs of lepers, and he eventually succumbed to the same *ugly* disease.

Albert Schweitzer, the theologian, philosopher, and physician, resolved at a young age to repay the world for the happiness it gave him. To do so, he set up a hospital in the remote jungles of Africa, where he took care of the very sick and invalid until he passed away at age 90.

Eleanor Roosevelt found her happiness by being a very outspoken advocate for many noble causes while her husband, Franklin Delano Roosevelt, was in office. Most notably, she was a vocal supporter of the African-American civil rights movement. After FDR died in 1945, she continued to work for human rights. Her path to happiness was through helping the disadvantaged in society.

Mother Teresa, the Albanian-born nun, founded the Missionaries of Charity to run dispensaries, mobile clinics, soup kitchens, orphanages, and schools, along with hospices and homes for people with AIDS, tuberculosis, and leprosy. Its members made vows of chastity, poverty, and obedience, as well as to give wholehearted free service to the poorest of the poor. The Mother derived her happiness by living amongst the poorest of the poor of Calcutta, India and helping them.

Audrey Hepburn, the film and fashion icon of Hollywood's Golden Age in the 1950s and early 1960s, likewise placed a great value on human happiness—both for herself and others. While she was enjoying great success as an actress in films such as *Sabrina, A Nun's Story,* and *Breakfast at Tiffany's,* she commented that, "The most important thing is to enjoy your life—to be happy—it's all that matters." However, while she was focused more on personal happiness as an actress, later in life, Hepburn gave up acting and devoted her time to UNICEF as a Goodwill Ambassador, helping impoverished children in the poorest nations. In this capacity, she worked in some of the most disadvantaged areas in Africa, South America, and Asia, helping people obtain food and medicines. She received the Presidential Medal of Freedom in 1992, shortly before her death at age 63.

You can find many other examples of people who gained their inner happiness through their own ideas or great works which contributed to the betterment of society. Their stories show that happiness does not just come from seeking pleasure—or sensual self-indulgence—a pursuit that gained its own name, *hedonism*. Instead, the kind of happiness attained by the individuals described above was far more enduring and came from contributing to the happiness of others.

The good news is there is no need or expectation for us to do anything spectacular to attain our share of happiness. Each human life has the built-in potential to find happiness and there are many different paths to reach this nirvana. No two minds will be alike in this pursuit. For one person, it may come from having a close-knit family with a caring spouse and loving children. Another person might find true fulfillment derived from the hours and days spent in a creative endeavor.

Many find happiness in their daily work and from hobbies they pursue on their own or with friends and by imbibing the beauty and grandeur of nature. Some people attain their happiness by doing hospital volunteer work or helping out the school programs or raising money for charitable events. A popular Chinese proverb expresses the ways to find happiness: "If you want happiness for an hour—take a nap. If you want happiness for a day—go fishing. If you want happiness for a year—inherit a fortune. If you want happiness for a lifetime—help someone else."

Are You Happy?

Since happiness is such a powerful and positive emotion and without it life becomes monotonous and miserable, let me ask you to reflect on your life and answer the question, are you happy? Your answer may capture not only how you feel now, but also the feelings and experiences of a lifetime, all in a word of *Yes* or *No*—You will have plenty of well-recognized reasons to expand on your one-word answer. Yes, I am happy with my life—I received a good education and developed a good career—My happiness comes from supportive parents—I am lucky to have a reliable spouse and wonderful children by my side—My belief in God and a good philosophy of life keep me happy and level-headed. Or, no, I am unhappy with my life—I cannot find a job—I cannot quit drinking—My wife left me with the children—I cannot quit smoking—I cannot get along with my siblings.

While looking back in life, for most people it would be a mixed bag of good and bad times, lucky breaks and unpleasant happenings, well-planned events and unexpected outcomes. Since life was not an even playing field, some would have the distinct advantages from the very beginning, especially with mental and physical health. There would be others who either did not get a good start in life or lost their accumulated assets through misadventures or misfortunes. Also, there would be an admirable group of people who built their house of happiness, despite heavy odds against them.

Harris Poll

A 2013 Harris Poll of 2,345 U.S. adults found that 77% were *generally happy* with their life. That is good news. For them, their inner satisfaction came from achieving what they desired in life, scoring high on positive relationships with family members, good connections with friends, and solid spiritual beliefs. Others achieved this goal by getting a good education, building a dependable career, engaging in community activities, helping out others in need, practicing their faith, or reaching out to the Almighty. There were also many others who attained their happiness knowing well the limitations of life and having the willingness to be satisfied with what life offered to them. All of these are highly commendable.

However, the same Harris poll revealed that only one in three were *very happy*, meaning the vast majority of people were missing out on this achievable goal. If you belong to this camp or a sense of helplessness prevails over you, now is the time to make the necessary steps, to make the rest of your life-journey more satisfying. The immediate reaction of most unhappy folks would be to look outward for easily identifiable causes—bad relationship with parents, a son with ADHD, a daughter with oppositional defiance, a spouse who changed markedly since the marriage, lack of education, living on a tight budget, not being connected with church, lacking in spirituality, and so on. All of them could be important, however, the search should be internal as well, to find out if there's anything wrong with the mental foundation. Can the bad relationship with parents be due to one's own greediness or jealousy toward siblings? Can the difficulty in handling one's child be because of a high level of stress at work? Can the marriage problems be caused by suspicions or obsessive traits of a partner? It is not only the mental disorders, but the *Mind Problems* too have the power to wear away the human happiness and bring on misery and calamities.

Happiness Reports

World Health Organization's Happiness Report identified that the mental illness was the single most important cause of unhappiness, significantly impacting an individual's capacity to lead a fulfilling life, which included the ability to study, work, and pursue leisure interests. The report did not specifically look into the subclinical disorders and significant *Mind Problems*. However, it is impossible to have a meaningful life in their presence, since they become constant irritants taking away the happiness.

The importance of happiness is recognized internationally, since it benefits the whole society, making life therein more peaceful and satisfying. In recognition of this, in July 2011, U.N. General Assembly passed a historic resolution inviting its member countries to measure the happiness of their people, so this information could be used to guide their public policies. The following year, the U.N. had a summit titled "Well-Being and Happiness: Defining a New Economic Paradigm" and chaired by the Prime Minister of Bhutan, the only country to have officially adopted *Gross National Happiness* instead of *Gross Domestic Product* as the main indicator of that country's development.

Over the next few years, World Happiness reports began to emerge using the data from Gallup World Poll, showing the level of happiness in all countries. The latest report identified the top five happy countries as Norway, Denmark, Iceland, Switzerland and Finland. The United States came in 14th, meaning there is lot of room for improvement even for the greatest nation in the world.

Dividends

Just being happy, is it not by itself a pleasurable dividend for genetically lucky people who live their life well? Will this state of mind allow those with it to live longer? Maybe! Andrew Steptoe, Director, Institute of Epidemiology and Health Care, University College London and colleagues assessed enjoyment of life in 9365 men and women with a mean age of 63 years. They found out that compared with the people who derived no enjoyment out of life, those who reported high enjoyment had lower mortality after adjustment for several variables. The results were published in the December 13, 2016 British Medical Journal online. The women in general and those who were married or cohabiting, well educated, wealthier, younger, and currently employed reported higher levels of enjoyment. Steptoe commented, "We found the more occasions on which people (reported) enjoying their lives, the lower their mortality over the next 6 to 7 years. Those who said they did not enjoy their lives at any time were the most likely to die."

In my private and professional life, I have come across people of various ages, cultures and socio-economic backgrounds, and have been fascinated by how some of them maintained a happy outlook, even when the odds were heavily against them. It may have been their healthy genetic inheritance or strong ability to maintain family relationships or a solid faith system or rich philosophy of life. Unfortunately, there were others who succumbed to unhappiness, living in a deep pit, and unable to climb out of it. Among them, there were even young people with healthy bodies and other distinct advantages in life, however still unhappy, since their minds were unhealthy. Also, there were others happy at one time, but lost it due to bad habits and unexpected misfortunes. The bottom line of it all, it is impossible to be happy unless the mind is healthy, devoid of not only mental disorders, but also any significant *Mind Problems*.

Certainly, the absence of mental disorders and *Mind problems* would not equate to happiness of human mind, however, with their continued presence, it would be impossible to build up a happy, meaningful life. The happy life would tremendously help each person to make the right choices in life, early on pertaining to education, career, and friends. Later on, it would concern about having a mate, establishing own family, and whether to have children or not. Other pivotal choices would involve deciding one's value system, personal habits, financial goals, philosophy of life, and the degree to which to assimilate spirituality, religion and God into one's daily life. Again, those with the healthy minds would keep on making good choices, and such choices would nourish the mind even more to keep it healthy and happy.

PART II

MIND PROBLEMS

CHAPTER 4
MIND PROBLEMS

I named several of the *Mind Problems* in the Introduction that have the unpleasant ability to shake up the foundation of the house of happiness and bring on ill health. There are several others too and each person needs to seek out what they are afflicted with by conducting self-examination. The *Mind Problems* like stress or anxiety, if continuously irritating, can easily become obvious to the victims and the danger will be in minimizing their importance. Those like greed or arrogance may miss out of the radar due to their infrequent appearances, needing much more introspection and insight to accept them as significant. Some people with envy or volatility may be forced to accept them as real problems only after certain setbacks in their life, like marriage in doldrums or facing legal embarrassment.

Any unusual behavior after a negative life event has to be watched for a significant *Mind Problem* or at times even for subclinical or clinical disorder. If the person who got a pink slip lost motivation to look for another job, may very well be suffering from a low-grade depression. Also, if any normally expected behavior took an unusual turn, it can be due the emergence of a significant *Mind Problem* or mental disorder. Such examples are if the culturally defined grief process took longer to resolve and made the person feel hopeless, or a mother after delivering the baby had difficulty in bonding with her little one.

Those with family history of mental illness have to realize that all the afflicted family members may not have the similar symptoms. With varying genetic penetration of major illnesses, some may inherit the full-blown illness, while in others can emerge with its milder versions or sometimes even with *Mind Problems*. It is not unusual, some to have an undue sensitivity to stress or in some others it manifests as a behavioral or addiction problem.

Goddess Lakshmi

A group of brave women of Lakshmipuram, fed up with the at-titudes and behaviors of their husbands vowed to bring an end to it. Led by their president Lakshmikutty, the village delegation approached Lakshmi, the wife of Lord Vishnu, to find a solution.

"Goddess Lakshmi, you are the goddess of wealth, fortune, and prosperity, and you have provided our husbands with plenty of it. However, we are unhappy since they are not only stingy with the mon-ey, but also make our daily lives miserable" said the president, opening up the Pandora's Box.

Encouraged by their leader, other women came forward with their own complaints—my husband came home drunk last night and yelled at me and children—my husband is jealous and will not allow me to go to any parties—my husband is obsessed with pornography—my husband is suspicious of me all the time—lazy, stubborn, arrogant, violent. My husband is narcissistic, a college graduate added. The list went on and on.

The Goddess looked at them sympathetically and pointed out, "These are the problems everyone has in their daily lives. This is a part of being a human being. This is the price you pay for living on planet earth."

The women were disappointed. Some were in tears. Touched by the weepy scene, the goddess agreed to grant just one request. The delegation was ecstatic, however in a quandary, since they felt all their complaints were important. They looked at their president to come up with a brilliant idea. Indeed, she had one! With a confident smile on her face, she asked, "Goddess, Lakshmi, would you be gracious to bestow on men, the pleasure of childbirth pain?" The group applauded the smartness of their president. Maybe this would teach them a lesson!

The Goddess was in conflict and reminded the delegation, in spite of labor pain, giving birth to a child was a beautiful privilege only women could have. "It is an important part of human life. It is an es-sential part of being a woman and no man can have it."

Lakshmikutty reminded the Goddess, they would still be glad to carry the baby in their wombs for the long months, they ask only to get rid of the pain and give that *privilege* to men! The goddess reluctantly agreed.

The womenfolk jubilantly returned to Lakshmipuram, spreading panic among the men. One by one the women became pregnant, their husbands yelling and cursing with labor pains. Finally, the turn of president Lakshmikutty came. Her salesman husband waited patiently next to the labor room, cursing his fate. However, he did not feel the pain. The baby was about to come out. Still no pain! All of sudden, everyone heard loud screaming from the neighbor's house.

At the end of story, the delegation of women went back to Goddess Lakshmi to rescind their request. The amused goddess agreed and reminded them that everything in life was set up in certain ways for a *good reason.* Is it this *reason* forcing the humans to accept any kind of despair as part and parcel of everyday life?

Religious Influence

In Hinduism, the concept of karma conveys that suffering is part of life, brought on by the thoughts and actions in this life or a previous life. In Bible, Peter wrote, "—who ever suffers in the body is done with sin." From Matthew came these powerful words, "Whoever does not take up their cross and follow me is not worthy of me." Religions generally encourage the followers to mortify their sins of flesh by fasting and abstinence; some groups even promote inflicting pain through self-flagellation. In some Christian countries the men carry huge wooden crosses through the streets on Good Friday, imitating the last journey of Jesus. In the Philippines, annually, the crucifixion is carried out to the extreme, in which penitents have real nails hammered to their palms and feet!

Evolutionary Impact

How much of the *ethos of toughness* brought on by the evolutionarily process on the human mind? The value of such toughness is expressed in popular sayings, "When the going gets tough, the tough get going." Did this instinctive desire derive from the principle of *survival of the fittest* which resulted in stronger members of a species surviving to pass on their genes to future generations and provided distinct advantages throughout human history? In the hunter-gatherer days, the tough men who returned home after hunting down large animals received celebratory welcome by others, and this quality was likely to appeal to women, primarily the gatherers. In ancient Rome, the gladiators who lived through blood-soaked spectacles became heroes and even sex symbols. And in medieval times, the strong ones became successful nobles and kings who were able to assemble and lead armies that helped them gain lands and become leaders of their people. Even today the bravado of young men running with bulls through the narrow streets of Pamplona, Spain, risking injury or even death brings them glory.

Every school age child is taught the tragic story of courage displayed by male passengers and crew members who obeyed the principle of saving women and children first, when the Titanic went down. By contrast, those who showed timidity or cowardice were shamed, such as when the Italian cruise liner Costa Concordia struck a rock formation, and ship captain Francesco Schettino abandoned the ship, leaving behind the crew and passengers, while 32 victims died at sea.

Psychoanalytic Clout

Psychoanalysts were always fascinated by the common *Mind Problems*, without calling them such, in their pursuit to understand the everyday psychic drama. However, they invested more emotional energy on internal mind events, paying less attention to externally observed happenings. It was much easier for them to understand the *stress* as an emotional experience alone and *anxiety* as the result of psychic trauma. The vibrant biological psychiatry was able to challenge their hazy thinking, arguing that there were *psychic* as well as *physical* symptoms due to *directly experiencing the traumatic event,* and this led to the emergence of PTSD diagnosis.

The school of psychoanalysis vastly influenced the understanding of *anxiety*, placing it under birth trauma, the banner initially erected by Freud himself, who called the birth "first experience of anxiety and thus the source and prototype of... anxiety" for the rest of the individual's life. In 1924, Otto Rank, his close colleague took it to even higher level and wrote—we are born into trauma and that trauma forms the "nucleus of the unconscious" and the essence of who we deeply are— The way an infant experiences this early separation from the mother becomes the foundation for all anxieties experienced later in the individual's life.

Today, even in its declining days, the clout of the psychoanalytical empire continues to influence our psychological and even the biological thinking. With the concept of Self, popularized by Carl Rogers, it will not be easy to accept the *Mind Problems* as significant, since they are glued closely to day-to-day life experiences. Taking a medication for daily stresses and anxieties will be unthinkable, since they are parts of human Self!

There is an eerie parallel in medicating *Mind Problems*, with the early days of antidepressant medications. In the early 1950s, when all the department chairmen were psychoanalysts and only sacred language conversed inside the inner chambers was Latin-psychoanalysis, it was hard for many of them to conceptualize depression as a clinical disorder. Andrew Solomon, Professor of Clinical Psychology at Columbia University later described depression as "flow in love." Siddhartha Mukherjee, the author of the book, The Emperor of All Maladies: A Biography of Cancer wrote in April 19, 2012 New York Times Magazine about the emergence of first antidepressant—Sea View Hospital at Staten Island observed the happy faces of men and women brought on by the anti-TB medication Iproniazid—those who consumed the 'feeling blue' drug Raudixin at Duke hospital carried the flows in Self-love (guilt, shame, suicidal thoughts), Love for others (blame, aggression, assaultive) and even Extinction of Love (lethargy, withdrawal, dullness).

Concerns

The notorious role of *Mind Problems* in causing social and health problems, and precipitate suicides and killings have already been described. The social problems can have serious personal, domestic, vocational and legal ramifications. The health problems can be as complicated as heart attack or stroke, even shortening the life span. In the Introduction, I highlighted the professional suicides; however, this tragedy could happen to anyone in similar situations. The killings exemplified through the school shooters, as well could emerge in other settings too.

There are several roadblocks on the way to recovery, for the *Mind Problems*. The major ones are about the tendency to deny or downplay them and the failure to recognize that a certain *Mind Problem* may have already attained a subclinical or clinical status. Concerns should be raised with any abnormal mental state; it did not matter if it was sadness or nervousness, irritability or anger—

- If it lasted a week or more
- If it bothered the person day and night, affecting sleep, appetite or sex drive
- If it made the person feel hopeless and helpless in life
- If it led to unhealthy coping methods
- If it resulted in domestic, health, vocational, or legal problems
- If caused by a life event, the emotionality was out of proportion to what caused it
- If it emerged in a family already afflicted with mental illness

Finding Relief

M. Scott Peck, the American psychiatrist and author of best-selling book, *The Road Less Traveled* reminded us that "Problems do not go away. They must be worked through or else they remain, forever a barrier to the growth and development of the spirit." The first and foremost step in managing any *Mind Problem* is to acknowledge it for what it has become and assess if any damage already happened due to it or from unhealthy coping methods.

Gandhi, considered a mind expert as well by many, said—What you feel and how you react to something is always up to you—you can choose your own thoughts, reactions, and emotions to most things in life—no one outside of yourself can actually control how you feel— you can incorporate this thinking into your daily life and develop it as a thought habit—a habit that can grow stronger and stronger over time. Eleanor Roosevelt, who became an important FDR administration's connection to the African-American population during the segregation era, echoed the same sentiment in a different way, "No one can make you feel inferior without your consent."

Just as the human body needs relief and help if it loses its health, the human mind needs the same if it lost its balance creating anxiety and confusion. When a significant event registered or a certain thought of importance intruded in, the inner chambers of mind would either handle it in a peaceful way or behave erratically if it lost equilibrium. If fitful, serenity has to be attained to get rid of this mental headache.

Most people with a *Mind Problem* can self-manage it by employing appropriate strategies- changes in life style—eliminating the unpleasant routines and adopting new ones—the person working in two jobs may have to cut down to one; carpooling instead of taking the long drive to work; if needed negotiating with the boss for better work hours—spending quality time with spouse and so on. Some people can find their relief sharing the stressful issues with family members and friends—picking up an enjoyable hobby—joining a health club—absorbing spirituality—imbibing the grace and wonder of nature—reaching out to the Almighty and so on. These strategies can work, especially for the *Mind Problems* of mild to moderate severity and if the mind not contaminated by unhealthy coping methods. There are several strategies available for those who have enough faith in human psychology and are not cumbersome to enforce.

Internal Dialogue

This technique can be employed when the mind is psychologically confused. It is the conversation, ego having with itself or as if each person has two minds—rational and irrational, communicating with each other to bring in inner peace. The rational, analytical part has to be truthful, and everything generated by it has to be based on facts to bring on a good resolution to the restless mind. Some people may find it easier by writing down their problems and solutions, seeing it on a piece of paper or computer screen providing better clarity.

Mindfulness

This practice lets the mind settle down and focus on current affairs, rather than running around in circles. It is done by educating the mind to live in the moment, paying attention to the present. Jon Kabat-Zinn, who founded the Mindfulness-Based Stress Reduction Program, defined mindfulness as "moment to moment non-judgmental awareness." It did not mean abandoning the past or disregarding the future.

Meditation

It refers to a broad variety of practices to allow the person to enter a deeper relaxed state of mind to get beyond the reflexive thinking, thus allowing bring on whatever is needed to subdue negativity. It means turning attention away from distracting thoughts and focusing on the present moment. It can be accomplished by turning attention to a single point of reference, focusing on the breath or bodily sensations, or on a word or phrase known as a mantra. This practice has been found effective not only in reducing stress but also managing medical problems like hypertension.

Mantra

In spite of its immeasurable vastness, the human mind cannot accommodate multiple thoughts, especially opposing ones, at the same time. The stressed person instinctively allows this to happen, making the mind to lose its equilibrium and result in psychological confusion. Based on this principle, the frequent recitation of a *mantra* word or phrase enables the person to get rid of the negative, troublesome thoughts. It can be done anytime, while driving to work anticipating a hard day's work ahead or lying restless in bed with disturbing thoughts or road rage building up, ready to burst out in the street or driving home to have a good time with family, however unable to let go the day's work.

Yoga

It is the practice to relax the body and mind, to uncover dysfunctional perception and cognition and to elevate and expand the consciousness beyond self. According to Natalie Nevins, a board-certified osteopathic family physician and certified Kundalini Yoga instructor in Hollywood, California. "The purpose of yoga is to create strength, awareness and harmony in both the mind and body—focus a lot—on preventive medicine and practices, and in the body's ability to heal itself." There are different schools of yoga, typically including breathing exercises, meditation, and assuming postures that stretch and flex various muscle groups. There have been several scientific studies supporting the physical and mental health benefits of yoga.

Professional Help

If the self-remedial measures did not succeed and the problem continued, professional help should be sought. This can be through practicing *relaxation techniques* of various kinds to calm down the body and mind, attending *anger management* to learn about the tools to manage this unpleasant aspect of their personality, *family therapy* helping the family to focus less on the member identified as ill and more on the family as a whole and *group therapy* in which people coming together to improve their life, learning from the therapist and other group members.

Psychotherapy

Leaving behind time-consuming psychoanalysis, psychotherapy has moved forward, establishing its reputation as an effective psychological treatment, allowing a distressed person to bring forth even their mind problems to a non-judgmental professional, getting clarifications and new direction in life. This skill is employed in different ways, some of the popular ones being psychodynamic psychotherapy, cognitive behavioral therapy, and supportive psychotherapy.

Medications

It should not come as a total surprise that medications used in the management of mental disorders could help controlling the *Mind Problems* as well. In this context, stress and burnout, feeling miserable and exhausted should be regarded as the younger brothers of major depression; vanity, arrogance, anger and aggression should be assessed for bipolar disorder; stubbornness, obsession, and jealousy should be evaluated for OCD. The innocent looking laziness if of recent onset may very well be a depressive disorder. However, there remains significant hesitation to take medication for *Mind Problems*, and even worse, reluctance by the health providers to prescribe them.

In the modern era of over-medication, this paradox is somewhat surprising. It is brought on by the fear of mind getting altered by chemicals. Even a *tough* person with a headache may not hesitate to take couple of Tylenol for relief. However, it is much different with *Mind Problems!* May be a drink or two to help out—smoking more—eating more, the comfort they seek eluding them, the problem only becoming worse.

The last several decades have witnessed the rapid advances in psychotropic medications in the management of mental disorders. Even though some physicians may prescribe them to their mild versions, there are no scientific studies conducted so far on their efficacy. So, it will strictly be a therapeutic trial, hoping at least some patients will benefit from it. This predicament was parallel to the early days of antidepressants, when the physicians were encouraged prescribing them only for severe depressions!

Prozac and similar medications have become the *broad-spectrum* meds of psychiatry, effective for a wide variety of conditions, akin to broad-spectrum antibiotics capable of fighting a wide variety of bacteria. The medical management of certain significant *Mind Problems* may involve mood stabilizers, anxiolytics and tranquilizers. The ultimate goal is to build a healthy and happy mind, not only by overcoming mental disorders, but the *Mind Problems* as well, and such a mind will empower each person to make the best choices in life, in reference to the family, relationships, education, career, marriage, children, personal habits, value system, faith, spirituality, and philosophy of life, among others.

CHAPTER 5
ANNOYING STRESS

God asked the first man and woman, "Did you eat the fruit that I told you not to eat?" They admitted to it. God pronounced judgement, "You will have to work hard and sweat to make the soil produce anything, until you go back to the soil from which you were formed." Immediately, the first couple was expelled from the Garden of Eden. From that time on, the humanity has been stressed out!

Mind Problem

Stress is a common *Mind Problem*, nobody escapes from its wrath and it is impossible to be happy in its irritating presence. Like a chameleon capable of camouflaging, it tricks those afflicted with it and manifests differently, depending on the age, gender and culture. The children and teenagers may be oblivious of it as an emotional experience, their temper tantrums and withdrawn behaviors often perplexing the parents. Generally, the elderly are capable of deflecting the kind of stress that bothered them earlier in life, using their learnt coping skills and having a better philosophy on life. Gender wise, the stress has the mysterious ability to drive men into silence, considering its revelation shameful, and women to chat more, to get the load off their chest!

The human culture has a multipronged impact on stress, in its emergence and perpetuation, as well as in its perception and management. To educate on these fascinating facets, the American Psychological Association has its own Journal titled, *International Journal of Stress Management*. It is well-recognized that cultural imprints are vastly different between the Western World with its more sophisticated lifestyle and the Eastern World embedded more in the traditional values. For the Westerners, if it was due to not having enough money to replace the broken washer and dryer or insurance jumping up after the

18-year-old crashed the family car or the single mother lost her high paying job due to outsourcing to Mexico, in the Eastern world, it could be about living in a crowded house with the in-laws or the mother-in-law continuously passing disparaging remarks about the cooking of her new daughter-in-law or the son would not marry the girl set up by the parents!

Across time, the nature of stress has changed even within the United States. It would be hard for those who lived a few generations ago, to imagine the kind of stresses the 21st century folks go through—the project set up for conference call with the company executives in Canada disappeared from the laptop—AAA would take an hour to come to the rescue due to high volume of calls—traffic blocked in the highway due to oil-spilling from a truck—the flight delayed due to terrorist threat—shooting at the nearby high school—son smoking e-cigarettes, on and on.

MSNBC Survey

In 2006, MSNBC did a series entitled *Stressed Out* and asked viewers what situations in their lives caused them the most stress. Here are some of their responses:

- So many home, child, work, self, and husband responsibilities
- Constantly feel like I'm behind, behind, behind
- Bills, bills, bills
- No job security; I don't know what I would do if I lost my job
- Dealing with the ever-changing emotions of two teenage daughters; they are like ticking-time bombs
- Disappointed with where I am with the goals I set
- I'm not enjoying my life
- I detest the constant pressure to survive
- Whatever happened to happily ever after? Is that just a fairy tale?

Stressful Jobs

Every year since 1987, Conference Board, the New York-based nonprofit research group has kept a tab on the job satisfaction in United States, those numbers tumbling down from about 61% to 52% during this time! CareerCast examined 200 professions to come up with a list of most stressful jobs and the following is their 2017 list with a stress score provided to each one of them.

- Enlisted military personnel: 72.74
- Firefighter: 72.68
- Airline pilot: 60.54
- Police officer: 51.68
- Event coordinator: 51.15
- Newspaper reporter: 49.9
- Corporate executive (senior): 48.56
- Public relations executive: 48.5
- Taxi driver: 48.18
- Broadcaster: 47.9

It should not come as a surprise, the jobs that required putting own life on the line or become responsible for others' lives came up at the top of the list. Even then, many people may not agree with the rankings completely and ask—Is it not being a taxi driver in a mega city more stressful than a commercial airline pilot? What about the air traffic controllers putting in nerve-wrecking hours each day to make sure no accidents occurred under their watch? How about the inner city teachers educating the children with developmental disorders and dealing with the dissatisfied parents, or the nurses working in the intensive care units day and night monitoring life minute to minute or the ER physicians making the lifesaving decisions around the clock? What about the single mother taking care of her young ones and holding an outside job at the same time, or the father working in two jobs to make sure his children have a brighter future?

The *Stress in America* Study emphasized that stress at work was less related to the type of job and more to the person's perceived sense of control at the work place. Is it not being President of United States the toughest, most stressful job in the entire world? If so, Ronald Regan seemed unfazed by it, while several other Presidents showed it out easily though their grey hair. The bottom line, it is hard to predict stress based on external factors alone. Internally, own personality with its stability and expectations played a major role in causing and perpetuating it. That would explain why some Police Chiefs working in the safety of their office rooms experiencing more stress than the cops carrying out the night patrols or TSA workers doing security checks at the airports developing more stress than the airline pilots.

Types of Stress

The Stress in America study also identified nearly 70 percent of Americans having experienced the physical and mental symptoms of stress and a quarter of them admitted to currently feeling under extreme stress, feeling fatigued, unable to concentrate or irritable for no good reason.

The most commonly identified stresses were the routine ones related to family obligations, school mandates, work responsibilities and everyday chores.

The stresses brought on by the everyday chores are harder to recognize, since the body may not give any clear signal of their arrival. They are also the ones most likely to be minimized too, even after becoming an irritating part of life and taking away the joy in living. However, many would be shocked, when these stresses boiling as if inside the tightly closed keg, suddenly got released and the hot water gushing out, burning them badly. Brown GW and group in a 1986 report published in the *Journal of Affective Disorders* pointed out the dangers of even these stresses, precipitating serious clinical disorders.

Less common, however, the more serious ones are brought on by the sudden, unanticipated negative life events such as losing the long-held job with a solid pension plan, spouse leaving after years of marriage that seemed normal or getting a deadly cancer diagnosis for an athletic nut, proud of his healthy body. Nobody can miss the punching power of this 9-foot gorilla, with high potential for mental and physical breakdowns. Even more dangerous can be from the traumatic events such as major accident resulting in serious injury, becoming a victim of physical or sexual assault, facing a natural disaster or living with the ravages of war wounding the psyche in unimaginable ways.

The concept of stress begs the question, are all the stresses bad for human beings? Maybe not. Some, if mild and short-lived may even be good! Such a stress, called *eustress* has the ability to heighten the sense of awareness, allowing to concentrate well on the task ahead. It can make the person resilient and better motivated to succeed. It would be more like stretching the muscles to keep the body healthy. Nobody has proved that watching a scary movie or riding rollercoaster or being shaken up by a creepy skeleton on Halloween night damaged the human psyche!

GAS

In 1936, the Hungarian-born scientist Hans Selye stumbled upon the idea of General Adaptation Syndrome (GAS) while searching for a new hormone! After his extensive studies on the stressed-out rats and human beings, he was recognized as a world authority on stress, and wrote, "Every stress leaves an indelible scar and the organism pays for its survival after a stressful situation by becoming a little older." Selye explained that the body passed through different stages of coping while facing stress—the immediate, universal response was an *alarm reaction* warning the body to prepare itself to put up a fight or run away from the scene as fast as possible. He pointed out that no organism could sustain this high negative-energy-generating condition too long and if it happened withered out easily, the body got *exhausted*, a sort of wear and tear. However, provided the human being was victorious in combat, a stage of *adaptation* would ensue in which resistance to stress was built with better coping skills.

Genetics

The National Institute of Mental Health defines stress as the brain's response to the demands placed onto it, and any change in and around the person has the potential to trigger this autonomous reaction. It may not be easy to visualize *stress*, a psychological conundrum brought on by a muddled up mind, as a biological event as well. However, there is plenty of evidence of the physiological underpinnings to this psychic drama. When stress is identified, the sympathetic nervous system goes into action without the permission of stressed individual, the commanding officers hypothalamus and pituitary send a signal all the way down to the top of the kidneys, asking the adrenal gland to release the stress hormone, cortisol. The chieftains, almond-shaped amygdala, prefrontal cortex, locus coeruleus and raphe nucleus, play modulating roles.

There is tremendous variation even among people of same age, gender and culture, how the stress emerges and how it is handled. Did the built-in personality characteristics make the difference, how the daily hassles impacted each person? Were those with healthy genes not likely to be bitten by the stress bug, and even if it happened, they had the increased ability to deflect the sting? Is it possible in those with a family history of mental illnesses, only some developing the full-blown illness or their subclinical forms, while others distressed with its milder versions only, like high sensitivity to stress?

A 2012 study conducted by Swedish researchers led by Timothy A. Judge analyzed the data from nearly 300 twins and concluded that the job stress was associated with the personality type and health, and that nearly 45% of the differences in personality type was due to genes. K.H. Song and colleagues used a different approach to understand the heritability of stress, passed from one generation to another. Their research with fruit flies concluded that stress could cause defect in one chromosome or group of chromosomes and this led to mutation of the chromosome, and passed on to future generations. They published their findings in the June 24, 2011 issue of *Cell*, with certainty that a similar inheritance process could go on in humans affected by stress.

Fight or Flight

In the story narrated earlier, the women of Lakshmipuram fed up with their husbands, approached the Goddess Lakshmi for help and learned a valuable lesson that everything in life was set up in a certain way, for a good reason! On a serious note, was the stress too set up by the nature for a good reason as a part of human life, to keep everyone on their toes and better prepared to face a larger crisis?

After Darwin brought forth his theory of evolution, it became a well-accepted dogma to explain the emergence of the natural events. Evolutionary thinking would go this way—primitive man when faced with danger from wild beasts or earthly disasters had to be heedful of his *fight-or-flight* response. He could stand and fight, or flee for safety. If this state of mind conditioned by the stress helped him and his family to survive, that was not bad at all.

Even today, the modern man confronted wild beasts while on hunting expeditions, however, there was no reason for *fight-or-flight*, having enough means to ensure his safety. He faced the natural disasters with the same mindset, with better scientific knowledge and advanced warning systems. Today's human mind is well aware of this cognitively, however, somewhere in the reptilian part of his brain, there are residues from the olden days, preventing its full comprehension. In those not well prepared, the old autonomous reaction emerged, what was extinguished simply resurfaced, some fought and succeeded, many more merely froze, unable to flee.

Measuring it

"Is it a good idea to measure stress?" asked Tom de Castella and Caroline McClatchey in the July 25, 2011, BBC News Magazine and they described the spectrum of gadgets available to do so, by checking the stress hormone levels, blood pressure, pulse rate and electrical conductivity of skin as indicators of emotional arousal. However, the experts have pointed out there was no consistency in, how people responded to stressful life events and trying to determine stress using the quantitative measures was flawed. Angela Patmore, author of *The Truth about Stress*, went even further, saying the self-testing was not just unreliable, it was harmful.

In 1967, psychiatrists Thomas Holmes and Richard Rahe, in an attempt to find out the significance of stress in causing illnesses, examined the medical records of more than 5,000 medical patients who were asked to tally a list of 43 life events. Holmes and Rahe's Stress Scale measured stress as the number of *Life Change Units*. Again the problem was, facing the same life event, the response could be highly varied from person to person, depending on their education, culture and psychological sophistication. A good example is that in certain cultures divorce can be more stressful than death of the spouse! Holmes and Rahe's Stress Scale has designated a score of 73 for divorce, while the death of spouse got the maximum 100.

DSM-5

The Posttraumatic Stress Disorder built on the foundation of trauma grew fast and furious, having received the continued push from the trauma experts, and helped by the dark winds from the Vietnam War. Acute Stress Disorder, the cluster of symptoms brought on by the exposure to actual and threatened death, serious injury or sexual violation, and the Adjustment Disorders as the development of emotional or behavioral symptoms with identifiable stressor(s) continued their timid journeys through the diagnostic manual.

What happens to the stresses commonly suffered without significant and identifiable stressors? The day-today stresses, the stress in taking care of the children, meeting the family needs within the budget, stress in the marriage, school and at work, should these mental headaches be placed on the backburner? They got lost amidst the scientific scrutiny, even though they could take an emotional and physical toll in the long run. The diagnostic manual still has a long way to go in its dealings with the stress.

Concerns

Is the stress a mental disorder? Dr. Richard Carlson, the psychotherapist and motivational speaker described stress as nothing more than a socially acceptable form of mental illness. However, there are mental health experts even today who prefers to keep stress on the peripheral blip of the clinical radar, needing rigid criteria to diagnose it, requiring major life events to generate it.

George Chrousos, MD, the scientist who spearheaded the conference on *The Profound Impact of Stress* in Washington, D.C., to educate the policymakers and public said that stress has been found to play a role in so many diseases from asthma, depression, and migraine flares to heart attacks, cancer, and diabetes. Medical scientists have specially studied the complex relationship between stress and the leading killer, heart disease

In a 2007 Journal of American Medical Association article titled, *Acute Emotional Stress and the Heart* by Janet M. Torpy, MD and colleagues wrote—Experiencing emotional or physical stress causes an increase in heart rate, elevation of blood pressure, and release of stress hormones—all these result in a greater workload for the heart—can cause a heart attack, sudden cardiac death, heart failure, or arrhythmias (abnormal heart rhythms) in persons, who may not even know they have heart disease. In its updated 2017 version of *Stress and Heart Health*, American Heart Association admitted more research needed to determine how the stress contributed to heart disease. However, emphasized that stress may affect the behaviors and factors that increased the heart disease risk—high blood pressure and cholesterol levels, smoking, physical inactivity and overeating—a stressful situation sets off a chain of events—body releases stress hormones—which may damage the artery walls—changes in the way blood clots, which increases the risk of heart attack.

Researchers in United Kingdom analyzed the data from 68,222 people who were followed for more than eight years to find the relationship between the stress and mortality and published their findings in the prestigious *British Medical Journal.* They paid special attention to the 12 percent of participants who died during the study period, after taking into account other factors that could have influenced the risk of death. What they found was surprising! Those with *high* level of stress symptoms had increased risk of death by 67 percent and in those with *moderate* symptoms the risk increased by 37 percent. The most astounding finding was even those with *low* level of stress had a 16 percent higher risk of dying, thus showing clearly, even this often neglected *Mind Problem* in minute doses, if sustained could kill people.

An analysis of even a larger pool of nearly 140,000 workers from three continents, whose health was tracked to find out the relationship to stress at work, revealed that those with the high-strain jobs were 22 percent more likely than their peers to suffer a stroke; this risk was as high as 33 percent for women holding the tough jobs. The results were published in a recent edition of the journal *Neurology.* According to a

2013 report by the Center for Disease Control/National Institute on Occupational Safety & Health 110 million people die every year as a direct result of stress. That meant seven people in every two seconds!

The destructive power of stress has to be understood not only by counting the number of strokes, heart attacks and other major health events, but also in the erosion in human relationships, number of marriage breakdowns, incidence of domestic violence, lessened job performance, increase in accidents due to absent mindedness and so on. It may be hard to measure all these in meaningful ways; however, what certain is that, ongoing stress of even mild nature can make the human life miserable and a hassle to put up with.

Burnout

Burnout is the culmination of excessive and prolonged stress, pushing the envelope to a much higher level, to a state of mental and physical exhaustion. By this time, the whole emotional turmoil may have been inching toward a clinical depression. However, many people would be reluctant to consider such a frightening possibility, preferring to hide behind a cloak of secrecy. David Ballard, the Head of the American Psychological Association's Healthy Workplace Program was quoted in a 2013 Forbes article on the signs of *Burning Out*:

- Emotional, mental or physical exhaustion
- Lack of motivation
- Frustration and cynicism
- Difficulty to concentrate
- Slipping job performance
- Interpersonal problems at home/work
- Not taking care of self
- Being preoccupied with work, when not at work
- Less satisfaction in career and home life
- Health problems, physical and mental

To expose the myth that burnout was simply a normal part of human life, Medscape conducted a survey of the U.S. physicians from more than 25 specialties. Their 2016 *Psychiatry Lifestyle Report* based on the data received from 15,800 physicians, brought forth the havoc of burnout among them. The survey strongly suggested that the burnout among U.S. physicians reached a critical level, exhibited through loss of enthusiasm for work, feelings of cynicism, and a low sense of personal accomplishment. The highest percentages of burnout occurred in the critical care, urology and emergency medicine, followed closely by the family medicine and internal medicine. A report published in *Time* magazine recently, of nearly 8000 surgeons who volunteered information admitted that their stressed mind state was among the strong predictors of major error during a procedure.

Tragedies

The most serious complication of stress and burnout among those who wore the white coat was suicide. Exposed to the cultural mantra, they were supposed to be tough while facing adversities, this group of well-educated men and women often denied or downplayed their *Mind Problems*, and even covered them up from their family members. The ultimate tragedy was some 400 U.S. doctors committed suicide every year; the rates higher than in the general population.

Michael F. Myers, M.D, author of the book, *"Why Physicians Die by Suicide: Lessons Learned from Their Families and Others Who Cared"* pointed out that "—we're living in an age of burnout; roughly 50% of U.S. physicians suffer from burnout." He described the burnout, "It is a state of emotional exhaustion, depersonalization (a lack of feeling for others), and a diminished sense of personal accomplishment. The burnouts by themselves are hazardous to health; however, more likely, many of these so-called burnouts may have already achieved a clinical depression status. With less stigma attached to the banner of burnout, many docs would rather hold onto it, rather than admitting they had a mental depression.

Pranay Sinha, a resident physician at Yale-New Haven hospital in 2014 wrote an opinion piece in New York Times, posing the question, *"Why do doctors commit suicide?"* According to him a key reason was the *ethos of toughness* that he described as "a strange machismo that pervades medicine." What is certain, this line of thinking negatively affects not only the medical people, but also the battle-fatigued soldiers, anxious first-responders, stressed-out police officers, and the public-at-large.

Under this culture of toughness, even admitting to have stress at work or home, nervousness while grocery shopping or meeting others, anger problem or jealousy in daily life would be seen a sign of weakness, and not revealing and putting up with it judged a sign of toughness. With this line of thinking, the anxiety during a job interview or fright after diagnosed with cancer or sorrow after losing a beloved pet would be considered normal parts of everyday life.

W. Clay Jackson of the University of Tennessee pointed out this physician problem in a presentation at the 28th Annual U.S. Psychiatric and Mental Health Congress at San Diego, CA in September 2015: "Professional licensure is not a talisman against depression and suicide; in fact, it may place one at a greater risk. Mental health is not a birthright of professionalism, but must be attended and maintained, as any aspect of our well-being." He went on to explain that burnout, characterized as a "loss of interest in work, a cynical mindset, and a low sense of accomplishment" played a major role in physician suicide. Though the symptoms were not enough for a clinical diagnosis of depression, they were serious enough to make a person to take own life.

Managing It

If the stress is anticipated, it may be possible to develop common-sense strategies to prevent it inflicting much pain. It can be about starting a job, buying a house, getting married, settling a loan, sending the teenager to college or preparing for a surgical procedure and so on. The strategic approach should be to avoid accumulating too many stress points—for example, postponing the buying of house at the same time of starting a new job, or delaying the marriage until the financial problems settled.

For those burdened by stress and burnout, the recognition that '*I am stressed out*,' '*I am burnt out*,' a proclamation of self-awareness is the first step towards recovery. With proper insight, most people could handle it on their own, especially if the problem was not too severe in nature. Some may even see this as an opportunity to change their routines in life, working less, developing better communication with others, rekindling contacts with old friends, seeking peace and comfort in the grandeur of nature, elevating spirituality to a higher level, seeking out the Almighty through prayer and meditation, picking up new habits, sleeping more, joining a health club, engaging in hobbies, practicing yoga and so on. In spite of the self-strategies, an American Psychological Association survey revealed that only 37 percent under stress thought they were doing very well at managing it. Many likely failed due to downplaying their problem or by using the wrong coping methods to overcome it.

Those who failed should seek out professional help. Psychotherapy can help charter a new direction in life, subduing the painful, sustained stress. William James, the American philosopher and psychologist said, "The greatest weapon against stress is our ability to choose one thought over another." The efficiency of this strategy would depend on, how much the stressed person believed it was not simply caused by a life event by itself, but also due to the *thoughts* about it. Since stress and burnout, unless properly managed, can lead to marriage breakdowns and family conflicts, such individuals will need appropriate counselling as well.

David Ballard suggested the following steps for the management of Burnout:

- Take relaxation seriously—Cultivate a rich non-work life
- Unplug—Set boundaries to communication technology when off work
- Get enough sleep
- Get organized
- Stay attuned to physical and mental symptoms of burnout
- Know, when it's you and when it's them. Internal problem v/s due to nature of work
- Figure out when enough is enough. If nothing worked, may be time to move on.

Medication Treatment

There are FDA approved medications for the Post-traumatic *Stress* Disorder; however, no such meds have been officially approved for the simple stress. Physicians often use antidepressants and antianxiety drugs for this purpose, for those who present to them with stress and burnout, considering these problems as the younger siblings of clinical depression. Some of them may have already become a depressive disorder, responding even better to the medications.

The arrival of Prozac in 1987 influenced the treatment landscape in major ways, due to their simplicity to administer, as well as better side-effect profile. The language of chemical imbalance reemerged with the renewed knowledge of serotonin by Eli Lilly scientists. The biochemical theory of depression that unfolded in early 1950s was reinforced by the new drugs. The distinct advantages of Prozac and similar meds, combined with their lack of lethality in overdose made it possible even for the family practitioners and internists to prescribe them in abundance, without the need to refer their patients to psychiatrists. By end of 1980s, Prozac itself had 40 million users, and this led to *Newsweek* to comment—"Prozac has attained the familiarity of Kleenex and the social status of spring water!"

Elizabeth Wetzel gave kudos to this pill in her book, *Prozac Nation*, explaining that before taking the medication, she was living "a computer program of total negativity, an absence of affect, absence of feeling, absence of response, absence of interest" and floated from one suicidal reverie to the next. A few weeks after being on Prozac, she described how her life was transformed. "One morning I woke up and really did want to live. It was as if the miasma of depression had lifted off me, in the same way that the fog in San Francisco rises as the day wears on. Was it the Prozac? No doubt."

Another group of medication that profoundly affected the treatment of stress and burnout was antianxiety meds, benzos, like Xanax, Ativan, Klonopin and Valium. They were found extremely useful for short term use, for those who did not have addiction problem. Even with the public fascination with these drugs and their widespread usage in psychiatry, many health practitioners still continue to downplay their role in subclinical disorders and significant *Mind Problems*, like stress and burnout. In our over-medicated society, this paradox is somewhat surprising! Even a mild headache is a headache and can be treated by the medication; however, stress or burnout, no way! How about moderately severe stress that lasted for weeks? Even with this, maybe psychotherapy, definitely not the medications! Many have missed out on their golden chance of recovery under these false pretenses.

CHAPTER 6
MISERABLE STATE

"*O*h, *darling, I've been so miserable.*" Earnest Hemingway who wrote these words in the 1926 novel *The Sun Also Rises* 'became miserable later in his life that tragically ended on July 2, 1961. There were other celebrities as well, who turned out to be miserable in their lives and some of them downplayed its seriousness and paid a terrible price for their miscalculation. Elvis Presley was one of them.

Elvis

This talented man, one of the best performers the world has ever seen, once confessed to his preacher "Pastor I'm the most *miserable* young man you've ever seen. I've got all the money I'll ever need to spend. I've millions of fans. But, I'm doing what you taught me not to do and I'm not doing the things you taught me to do." Unable to redeem himself from his miserable state, he collapsed on the floor of his bathroom. The *King* who downplayed his problem as only *miserable* died at age of 42 engulfed in deep misery. The man who took comfort in believing that he consumed only the medications prescribed by physicians and not street drugs, died from too many pills in his system—fourteen, with ten in significant quantity!

Lincoln

More than a century earlier, Abraham Lincoln wrote a letter to John T. Stuart, his law partner—"I am now the most *miserable* man living. If what I feel were equally distributed to the whole human family, there would not be one cheerful face on the earth. Whether I shall ever be better I cannot tell; I awfully forebode I shall not. To remain as I am is impossible; I must die or be better, it appears to me."

William Henderson, another law partner described Lincoln, "His melancholy dripped from him as he walked." However, this towering personality who did not hide his problem, successfully navigated through the political arena, praised by the abolitionists as a champion for human liberty, Republicans proudly linking his name to their party, and even Democrats would not hesitate to quote him as a hero. The countless books and Hollywood movies always displayed him in high favor. Abraham Lincoln lived in an era without effective treatments for melancholy. However, he acknowledged his problem and in spite of it, made himself one of the greatest presidents of the United States.

Miserable State

Both Elvis and Lincoln described their condition as *miserable*, however, they had distinctly different problems. While the Presley's was a *Mind Problem* initially, that escalated to a prescription drug dependence and finally made him collapse under its weight, the President with a clinical disorder thrived in spite of its aggravation. Winston Churchill who had episodes of mental paralysis that forced him to spend long hours in bed with no energy, called his miserable state as his *Black Dog*. Kay Redfield Jamison of John Hopkins University School of Medicine described these mood changes as the *Charnel House*—a vault where human skeletal remains are stored—a place of death and destruction. Those who recognized the gravity of their problem and sought help, survived. Those who downplayed it simply perished.

According to the National Institute of Mental Health, clinically significant miserable states afflicted about 6.7 percent of U.S adults each year, running rampant within the family confines. Twin studies have suggested heritability of 40 to 50 percent, and the family studies indicated a two to threefold increase in lifetime risk of developing it among the first-degree relatives. It is not unusual even in families loaded with genetic depression, only some family members show all its classical symptoms, while others may come down with its subclinical forms or manifest it as a significant *Mind Problem*.

Repeat Advents

The miserable state, substantial or miniscule, often appeared as if a burglar breaking in, holding hostage, spreading fear and anxiety, discouraging the homeowner from eating and sleeping, preferring to stay put for about six months, unless the cop called in. The benevolent officer, a health provider, if talks to the burglar to leave, he may do so reluctantly. If a chemical was pushed in to make him depart, for mysterious reasons, the intruder would leave only after three weeks! Even after such exit, unfortunately, one cannot rest without concern, since the same burglar may very well return. As in the case of brain seizures, one entry paves the way for the next one, unless the homeowner takes necessary precautions.

According to the American Psychiatric Association, 50 percent of those who recovered from the first episode of depression would have one or more additional bouts in their lifetime. After the second one, the risk rapidly climbs up to as high as 80 percent. In this psychological-biological chase, some break-ins can be serious, in others the burglar only causes some commotion, more like a *Mind Problem*.

Sense of Humor

It is hard to have any sense of humor, when under the spell of the burglar. They are adversaries with deep dislike to each other. However, some brave souls hold onto this golden thread, to prevent going down the drain. Syndicated columnist Art Buchwald wrote about his miserable moods and difficult childhood in his memoir *Leaving Home*. His mother was forced to check into a mental hospital after he was born and he grew up in orphanages and foster homes. After he recovered from his miserable moods, he joked about it, "During both my depressions, I contemplated suicide. My main concern about my death was that I would not make the New York Times obituary page. I was sure it would be just my luck that Charles de Gaulle would die on the same day and all the space would be taken up with tributes to him." He and his colleague Bill Styron had mental breakdowns within months of each other and they teased about whose was stronger, "I claimed that mine had been a 9.9 on the Richter scale, and he said I had suffered nothing more than a rainy day at Disney Land. What I didn't tell him was that I planned to have Isaac Stern play at my funeral."

Almost Depressed

His melancholy dripped from him as he walked—If the mental condition was that bad, nobody would miss it. However, being a disorder of varying grades, some have only a mental fever and if so, it would be easy to ignore it, since the clinical thermometer hardly registered it. According to Shelley Carson, a professor at Harvard University and co-author of the book, *Almost Depressed: Is My (or My Loved One's) Unhappiness a Problem,* many people suffered from it, in other words, they were *almost depressed*. In a recent article for CNN Health, Carson shed more light on this in-between unpleasant state. "Research suggests that as many as 12 million people in the United States may be suffering from low-grade depression symptoms that are not severe enough to warrant clinical treatment." These symptoms are:

- Inability to enjoy things that used to be fun
- Easily irritated and overreacting to minor incidents
- Regularly finding excuses to avoid socializing
- Going through the motions and feeling like each day a struggle
- Feeling overstressed, thinking will never catch up with all to-do.

Still, not significant enough to warrant clinical treatment! Carson went on to say, while being *almost depressed* was not considered a clinically treatable mental health condition, that certainly did not make it any less important to address. "At Harvard Medical School, we have been investigating the effects that *almost depression* and other subclinical conditions can have on an individual's quality of life. People who are almost depressed report a number of issues, including lower job satisfaction, lower satisfaction with their marriage and other personal relationships, more anxiety issues, less control over their lives and lower overall well-being than people who do not fall into the almost depressed range. Research indicates about 75 percent of cases of low-grade depression will devolve into full-blown major depression if they are not recognized and arrested."

Robert H. Pietrzak at the Veterans Affairs Connecticut Healthcare System and group studied *subclinical depression* in 34,000 U.S. adults and published their findings in a 2013 issue of *Psychological Medicine*. They found that more than 11 percent classified with it at the beginning of the study later developed more serious depression. Keep in mind the common *Mind Problems* were only a step behind the subclinical ones, having the punching power to hurt the victims on their own, also with the risk of growing up in size to a clinical disorder. In 2008, Pim Cuijpers, Professor Vrije University, Amsterdam and colleague measured the economic impact of minor depressions and found that the total costs of them were comparable to the major depressions, since they were more prevalent.

Even today, many in the public struggle with varied concepts of mood irregularities, wondering what exactly they are afflicted with. Some would ask themselves, as the title of Carson's book—*Is My (or My Loved One's) Unhappiness a Problem?* Being miserable and unhappy, are they not a part of normal day-to-day living and nothing more than that. Unfortunately, there would be some mental health practioners too in their camp!

Tired and Exhausted

Physicians often hear this complaint in their office room—I feel tired all the time—I feel exhausted. Some docs would ask them, if they were physically or mentally tired, exhausted. It is not easy to separate the two, many patients answering—I do not know. In reality, most people should be able to make this distinction, if they practiced well, paying close attention to their feelings and sensations. It will come with practice, using the trial and error strategy. Of course, there are telltale signs for the mental exhaustion, especially if it is approaching a clinical state of depression. Feeling hopeless in life or having suicidal thoughts are always part of a mental state.

However, it can coexist with a medical disorder, making it harder to separate. Such examples would be hypothyroidism or anemia manifesting with a clinical depression.

Grieving the Loss

In 1915, Freud published his monumental essay, *Mourning and Melancholia*, which outlined the psychodynamics of grief and distinguished between the mourning for a dead loved one and depression. Everyone held onto this cherished view, since grieving was considered a culturally defined, healthy mental process, to deal with the loss of a loved one. Occasionally, grieving got out of control and such person behaved abnormal during this solemn period of *six weeks* puzzling the onlookers!

The 2002 research by George A. Bonanno suggested that normal grief could last up to 6 months. Six months! How about 18 years? Longfellow, the 19th century American poet lost his wife Fanny in a fire, devastated, he never fully recovered. He wrote, "Every man has his secret sorrows which the world knows not; and often times we call a man cold when he is only sad." In the sonnet *The Cross of Snow* written eighteen years later to commemorate her death he revealed, "Such is the cross I wear upon my breast. These eighteen years, through all the changing scenes, and seasons, changeless since the day she died."

The diagnostic work group of the recent diagnostic manual of American Psychiatric Association was asked, "Is Grief a Major Depressive Disorder?" The very fact such a question raised at all surprised many, since the grieving was considered a normal adaptive process. If any unanticipated abnormal behavior emerged, yes, then only a clinical disorder would be complicating it. The term *funeral mania* was used to explain when a person behaved happy instead of sad on this distressing occasion! It could happen from the stress itself in a genetically predisposed person for bipolar disorder or its smaller mind versions, or from the sleep deprivation during those hectic days. Certainly, the substance abuse has to be ruled out.

If the grieving confined to the culturally defined limitations, would it need treatment? No! However, the expectations are raising—Well, doc, can I have sleeping pills to help me during this time? How about a supply of Xanax or valium?

Managing Misery

Author Brian Roberts published an article in 2015 in the *Huffington Post* titled, *"8 Ways to Stop Feeling Miserable and Start Being Happy."* He wrote, "We all have our bouts with the blues. You know, those times you just want to sit in bed all day, covers overhead, door locked shut. We've all been there. Being miserable is, well no fun." The ways he proposed to overcome such feeling:

- Stop isolating yourself
- Stop being a people pleaser
- Stop comparing yourself
- Start living
- Start talking to yourself
- Be bold
- Be real
- Start believing

Each expert may have his or her rules for redemption from the miserable state of mind, what important to keep in mind, some of the general ones can very well be helpful to you, however, you also have to be creative to come up with your own healthy strategies, depending on your age, education, career, family circumstances and living situation.

Similar to stress, the biggest mistake in the management of miserable feeling is downplaying its significance. Any such mind state, if it lasted a week or more and affected sleep, appetite or sex drive should be considered significant. If the self-remedial measures did not succeed, the professional help should be sought, which could be psychotherapy or medications, or a combination of the two—medication to correct the uneven brain chemistry and psychotherapy to paint the miserable mind in brighter colors.

Medications

What! Consuming a pill to get rid of the miserable feeling? Is it not feeling sad and being miserable, part and parcel of everyday human life? Did not a wise man say it was *flow in love*? Or was it a filling of an *existential vacuum* as described by Austrian psychiatrist Viktor Frankl or *inability to construct future* noted by American psychologist Rollo May. Experts entrenched in the humanistic, cognitive and psychodynamic concepts of sadness expressed their views, as the six blind men from Hindustan who touched the elephant and came up with their own versions about the animal!

Major events unfolded in early 1950s threw away the old hypotheses and allowed a new chemical theory to emerge. Two U.S. doctors travelled to Germany to learn about the anti-TB effects of a drug, first synthesized by two Ph.D. candidates in Prague as part of their doctoral requirements, and brought it back for further analysis. Finding out the drug, a monoaminooxidase inhibitor (MAOI) had good anti-TB activity, initially the human testing was carried out in the population of a Navajo reservation, where tuberculosis was endemic.

Encouraged, the next venue selected for testing was Staten Island's Sea View Hospital in New York. Only those T.B. patients with a poor prognosis were initially treated, nevertheless, their improvement was impressive. *Time* magazine proclaimed, "Never in the age-long history of tuberculosis had there been such excitement about a new treatment for the white scourge."

The researchers also noted "a subtle general stimulation... the patients exhibited renewed vigor and indeed this occasionally served to introduce disciplinary problems." A journalist wrote that the wards typically glum and silent, with moribund, lethargic patients were "bright last week with the happy faces of men and women." When *Life* magazine sent a photographer to the hospital to investigate—patients could no longer be found lying numbly in their beds—They were playing cards or dancing in the corridors!

Interestingly, a seemingly unrelated scenario took place at Duke Hospital, where it was observed that patients who ingested the medicine reserpine for hypertension came down with mental depression. Putting the two events together, the scientists concluded that the Sew View medication MAOI increased a certain enzyme and alleviated depression, while the Duke medication drained the same enzyme, resulting in depression! For the first time in human history, a profoundly different way of thinking about the mental depression emerged, directly challenging all the psychological and social theories prevailing at the time. The birth of biological psychiatry was taking place that eventually led to the fading away of psychoanalysts.

Another encouraging piece of news came from Munsterlingen asylum in Switzerland, where the scientists seeking a treatment for schizophrenia came across a drug, which made that mental illness worse, however, improved the mood of depressed patients. This was the introduction of tricyclic antidepressants, described by some as a *miracle cure* for depression. Another glamorous chapter was added to the book of psychopharmacology. This excitement reemerged in mid-eighties by the discovery of Prozac.

Depression attained certain respect, having been discussed in the media without hesitation and some celebrities revealed their inner pain without inhibition. However, the struggle to decide at which point the medications should be introduced into the treatment, continued. Should it be provided to only those with severe despondency? A generation of psychiatrists were even educated that more symptoms the patient had, more biological the disease was, and if so, more likely to respond to the medications.

Today, the patients with even mild and moderate depressions receive antidepressant treatment with or without psychotherapy. However, the hesitation to prescribe them to those with subclinical disorders continue. With this scenario, the *Mind Problems* are a total loss! Headache is a symptom and can be managed by medications; however, don't mess up the brains of those who have only mild miserable states! Many suffer from the consequences of this unfortunate double standard, and human lives have been lost as the result of it.

CHAPTER 7
NERVOUS TENSION

The Danish philosopher Soren Kierkegaard described the mind state of nervousness and apprehension as *Dizziness of Freedom,* since it inhibited the freedom in thinking and constrained the normal human behavior. It clouded the human mind, making it hard to see through the hazy smog, at times even paralyzing it, making the person blind temporarily to reality. The gentle, blue ocean waters could turn turbulent even without winds, and occasionally these same tranquil waters would be blasted out by the deeply held down psychic volcano with no warning signs.

Blast of Fear

On a sunny, spring morning in 2004, Dan Harris, the ABC News correspondent and the anchor for Nightline suffered an embarrassing on-air panic attack, freaking out in front of five million people, while filling in on *Good Morning America*, anchoring the news updates at top of each hour. Harris says of his attack "I had done this job plenty of times before, so I had no reason to foresee what would happen shortly after the co-hosts, Diane Sawyer and Charlie Gibson, tossed it over to me for my brief newscast: I was overtaken by a massive, irresistible blast of fear. It felt like the world was ending. My heart was thumping. I was gasping for air. I had pretty much lost the ability to speak. And all of it was compounded by the knowledge that my freak-out was being broadcast live on national television. Halfway through the six stories I was supposed to read, I simply bailed, squeaking out a—Back to You."

Different Categories

Dan Harris came through his embarrassing blast of fear unscathed. With no respect for its victim or the arena in which it emerged, these panic attacks did not care if the person was talking to millions of people on the TV or driving on the safest bridge in the world or shopping for the baby formula at the corner store or attending the Sunday services at the neighborhood church. Because of the chest hurting and heart galloping, those who experienced it for the first time likely would fear a heart attack or some such catastrophic event. The bull has gotten out of control, running all over the arena, hitting whatever it can. The driving force may be psychic, however, what comes out is mostly physical—sweating profusely, shaking like a leaf, filled-up lungs unable to hold any more air. The mind terrified of losing control, going crazy, or drop dead! The full-blown attack would get plenty of attention from the onlookers, calling 911 and anxiously waiting for the arrival of paramedics.

Many with anxiety did not have such blasts out of fire, instead had a tenacious mental headache, interfering with their everyday life. Feeling on the edge all the time, having somatic and sleep problems, such a person is looked down in society as the one without gumption. There would be others with unnecessary anxiety in places that did not require it, as traveling in a bus or riding in train or flying in a plane, or even being inside a half-empty grocery store.

Some children develop phobic anxiety, terrifying them, maybe after seeing a spider in the attic or a rattle snake on the television screen or hearing the horror story of a dental procedure. Some find thunder and lightning too much to bear, and learn to avoid elevators and closed spaces to prevent a disaster and will not use the public toilet loaded with germs! Others will not even get into shallow waters for the fear of drowning or dare to look down from a tall building for the fear of falling.

Social anxiety is a common phenomenon, preventing its victims achieving their full potential. It may begin as shyness, coming out in the full form in teenage years, forcing them not to raise hand in the classroom, avoid meeting new people or even give up eating in public. Fearful, they avoid social situations as much as possible; if it is not possible, endure it with great distress.

Anxiety disorders affect millions of people, making their own lives and also of their loved ones miserable. Since it is not easy to put up with a person who constantly anxious, sympathy likely to dry up easily, leading to arguments and skirmishes within the family. Kids with it suffer through poor grades and lack of age-appropriate social relationships, frustrating the parents and teachers. With the general hesitancy to seek help even for the disorders that have attained clinical stature, its milder versions, the *Mind Problems* often get a pass, often suffering in silence.

It's Biology

Anxiety is a dominant psychological state of mind, however the biology of brain plays a significant role in its induction and perpetuation. Scott Rauch, Professor of Psychiatry at Harvard Medical School reviewed the advances neuroradiology field had made in understanding the neural circuitry system, and implicated locus ceruleus and septo-hippocampal structures. The circuit goes haywire when the anxiety erupts. Other researchers have focused on the amygdala and its interconnected pathways on their role in triggering the flight or fight response, in which rational thinking and reasoning may not always be able to block the earlier primitive processing. It was like an alarm set up to find an intruder and when the cops arrived, it turned out to be a false alarm!

Complications

Those with undue anxiety and constant nervousness miss out on the highly positive emotion of happiness that adds color, excitement and energy to daily living. Forced to live with this limitation, such people get haunted by their perceived weakness, unable to enjoy even the best times in life and personal victories. This nervous condition, even when well-below a clinical disorder, has the ability to make life miserable. Adam Spira from John Hopkins Bloomberg School of Public Health and group reported that such subclinical disorders in older

adults were associated with higher levels of sleep disturbance and social dysfunction and published their findings in the 2008 *Journal of
Geriatric Psychiatry and Neurology*. A study by Neeraj Agarwal from
University of Utah School of Medicine and group found a relationship between subclinical anxiety and hypertension, and published their
findings in 2012 *Internet Journal of Cardiology*.

It is not unusual for those with anxiety disorders to self-medicate
with alcohol or prescription drugs. A recent three-year study of 34,653
Americans published in the *Archives of General Psychiatry* by James M.
Bolton of the University of Manitoba, Winnipeg and his team showed
the dangers of such behavior, 13 percent with anxiety disorder who
used alcohol to manage their problem developed significant alcohol
problems. The same trend was revealed in those who self-medicated
with drugs.

Another major complication of the unmanaged anxiety is the clinical depression to make the lives of the victims even more miserable.
They can be become inseparable dancing partners with a special affinity
for each other. The dance may very well begin solo through the social
anxiety or panicky feeling, but the depression would join in and the
band keep on playing melancholic songs. At times, they both would
dance ferociously with hardly any separation between them. The dancing partners did not even have to be fully mature adults in the clinical
uniforms to inflict psychic pain. A 2001 study published in *Archives of
General Psychiatry* by Professor Murray B. Stein of University of California, San Diego and group clearly showed a high risk for depression
in adolescents and young adults with the social anxiety and suggested
such with other anxiety states as well.

Too Much Worry

Worrying! Is it not supposed to be a part of normal day-to-day living experience designated for the humans from the time they put foot
on earth? If so, why make such a big deal about it? True. Even some
mental health experts would consider worrying a normative psychological state. However, what if it became persistent, a daily annoying experience, interfering with a person's day-to-day functioning? At what
point would it become significant and no more a simple worrying?

Some people seem worried all the time, sometimes, even when there was little or no reason to worry about, worrying about just getting through the day, their mind-engine programmed in a negative mode and could only visualize things going badly. Even if this feeling only came on while talking to a neighbor or attending a family get-together, it still could erode self-esteem easily, especially if its effects—shaky voice or trembling hands visible to others.

Guy Winch, a psychologist and author explained the differences between worry and anxiety in *Psychology Today*:

- Worry is in our heads and anxiety in our bodies
- Worry tends to be specific while anxiety is more diffuse
- Worry is verbally focused while anxiety includes verbal thoughts and mental imagery
- Worry often triggers problem solving but anxiety does not
- Worry creates mild emotional distress, anxiety can create severe emotional distress
- Worry is caused by more realistic concerns than anxiety
- Worry tends to be controllable, anxiety much less so
- Worry tends to be a temporary state but anxiety can linger
- Worry doesn't impact our professional and personal functioning; anxiety does
- Worry is considered a normative psychological state while anxiety is not

In spite of those distinctions brought out by the author, the demarcations separating the two are far less clear. Worry in our heads and anxiety in our bodies! Really? Both came out of the brain and have the ability to cause bodily symptoms. Did the worry trigger problem solving, but anxiety not? Of course, it would depend on their intensity. Excessive worry easily merged to an anxiety disorder, even experts would find it hard to separate them.

Mystery thriller writer Arthus Somers Roche described worry as a "thin stream of fear trickling through the mind. If encouraged, it cuts a channel into which all other thoughts are drained." Leo Buscaglia, the author and motivational speaker also known as 'Dr. Love,' said, "Worry never robs tomorrow of its sorrow, it only saps today of its joy." Dale Carnegie, the guru of self-improvement, explained "Our fatigue is often caused not by work, but by worry, frustration and resentment."

Jason Moser, the Michigan State University researcher pointed out the negative consequences of worrying, "It's something we do over and over again, without much resolution, and it's typically of the worst-case scenario of the future." He went on to say, "There's always an element of uncertainty, always an element of catastrophe. Unlike fear, which has a more pin-point able source, people worry over an amorphous, future uncertain threat—something bad that might happen." Erma Bombeck, the American humorist, described, "Worry is like a rocking chair: it gives you something to do but never gets you anywhere." Winston Churchill once said, "When I look back on all these worries, I remember the story of the old man who said on his deathbed that he had a lot of trouble in his life, most of which had never happened."

It is in human nature to be concerned about the mundane problems affecting health, money, family and so on, thus helping to formulate sensible plans in solving them. According to Harold Stephen, the American author, "A worried person sees a problem, and a concerned person solves a problem." The concern would be a notch below worry, may be about the low grades of the son, preoccupation of the daughter with video games or about broader issues as protecting endangered species or cleaning up the environment. Some people worry in an obsessive way, this kind of worry has OCD traits painted all over it.

Managing it

Henry Ford found the answer to his worry and said, "I believe God is managing affairs and He doesn't need any advice from me. With God in charge, I believe everything will work out for best at the end. So what is there to worry about?" Since worry once started can gallop forward as an uncontrolled stallion, it is important to recognize it for what it is, without distorting the facts. Dr. Edward Hallowell, author-psychiatrist, encouraged the worriers to find out more information about the issues troubling them to make sure that it was correct, as well as sharing the concerns with someone else. Another step recommended was to take care of the brain by sleeping enough, getting exercise and eating healthy. Hallowell encouraged worriers to get regular doses of positive human contact such as a hug or a warm pat on the back.

Huffington Post quoted Moser and Christine Purdon at the University of Waterloo on the common positive traits shared by people who managed their worries successfully.

- They focus on the present, rather than be bogged down by things that have yet to happen
- They practice mindfulness, to steer focus away from hypothetical issues that might only develop down the road
- Their brains actually function differently in a worry-inducing event, unlike the worriers who have a really hard time putting a positive spin on difficult situations
- They're more willing to take chances, more willing to test out solutions to a problem even if a bad outcome is possible
- They have a sense of perspective
- They get to the root of their worry, since worrying can take the person away from the immediate issue
- They don't stop **worrying**; they just designate time for it. Like reserving a 15-minute time where you can just think and ponder about your worries on your own; using the same *worry chair* each day
- They have confidence they can handle whatever comes at them
- They have the ability to see positive outcomes in seemingly bleak situations
- They ask themselves the right questions. It was suggested that the worriers could help themselves by asking: Is it my problem? Do I have any control over it? Have I already done everything about it that I can? How imminent it is?
- They know how to perceive their negative emotions and use the emotions to make informed decisions

American journalist Scott Stossel points out, "There are lots of things, including changing the kind of inner dialogue that can mitigate anxiety. And yes, these are people who have the glass half-full and glass half-empty, and I'm afraid the glass is going to break and I'll cut myself on the shards."

Eknath Easwaran, the spiritual teacher and author of the books on meditation, came with his answer, "As meditation deepens, compulsions, cravings, and fits of emotions begin to lose their power to dictate our behavior. We see clearly that choices are possible: we can say yes, or we can say no. All we are is the result of what we have thought."

Twenty-four hundred years ago Plato educated his followers, "Nothing in the affairs of men is worthy of great anxiety." Epictetus, the philosopher born as a slave, professed on the fallacies of anxiety saying, "Man is not worried by real problems so much as by his imagined anxieties about real problems." Charles Spurgeon, 19th century British Preacher, stressed on the anxiety's profound negative consequences saying, "Anxiety does not empty tomorrow of its sorrows, but only empties today of its strength."

In spite of the experts' attempt to draw a distinction between worry and anxiety, from a practical point of view, the separation is on a very thin ice. The recognition that *I am a worrying anxious person* can be the first step towards redemption. If mild to moderate and not sustained, most people can handle it on their own. Some may see this as an opportunity to change their routines in life, working less, developing better communication with spouse, rekindling with old friends, elevating spirituality to a higher level, seeking out the Almighty through prayer and meditation, or picking up new habits by sleeping more, joining a health club, engaging in hobbies, practicing yoga and so on.

Many others may try to spend more time in nature to recuperate from the stresses and anxieties, perhaps by fishing or playing golf or simply watching the beauty and grandeur of the world around. Henry David Thoreau, best known for his book, *Walden*, a reflection upon the simple living in natural surroundings pointed out that "There are moments when all anxiety and stated toil are becalmed in the infinite leisure and repose of nature."

However, if it became persistent, whether it was clinical, subclinical or part of a *Mind Problem*, would need professional management to make life happy. David D. Burns of Stanford University School of Medicine and the author of the best-selling book, *Feeling Good: The New Mood Therapy*, pointed out, "People who are prone to anxiety are nearly always people-pleasers who fear conflict and negative feeling like anger. When you feel upset, you sweep your problem under the rug because you don't want to upset anyone. You do this so quickly and automatically that you're not even aware you're doing it." However, believers in the biology of anxiety may not agree with this simplistic view by Burns.

Medications

The 20th century witnessed the emergence of medications to control anxiety, which was the exclusive playground of psychoanalysts. Barbital (Veronal) was discovered in 1903 as a hypnotic and almost a decade later phenobarbital (Luminal) emerged as a sedative-hypnotic. These drugs were not a match for Meprobamate (Miltown) that caught the public imagination and rapidly became the first blockbuster psychotropic drug in American history. Within a year of its launch in 1955, as many as 1 in 20 Americans had used it! However, the huge concerns over the safety and addiction potential led to their slow disappearance, to be replaced by the benzodiazepines.

The credit to the invention of benzodiazepines goes to Leo Sternbach who grew up Abbazia, then part of the Austro-Hungarian Empire. With a doctoral degree in organic chemistry from the University of Krakow, he joined Hoffmann-LaRoche in Switzerland. However, the Second World War changed his life dramatically, when all the firm's Jewish scientists fled Europe. Sternbach arrived in United States in 1941 at La Roche's new research facility in Nutley, New Jersey. His initial project to duplicate Wallace Laboratories Miltown tranquilizer, a popular drug then, did not succeed, and his own bosses urged him to move on to the research antibiotics. However, he pursued in his search to find a tranquilizer better than Miltown. The rest is history.

Sternbach and his colleagues invented Librium, which hit the market in 1960, followed shortly by Valium. These anti-anxiety drugs rapidly gained popularity among the medical professionals, as a major improvement upon the dangerous drugs used then, to reduce the psychic tension. Valium went on to become the Western world's most widely prescribed anxiety medication and first drug to reach $1 billion in sales and helped Roche to become a pharmaceutical industry giant.

The 1960s was a unique decade for United States, defined by a gruesome war and political assassinations, with Valium adding to the mystery of that time. Rolling Stones 1966 hit song, *Mother's Little Helper*, said it all, "Mother needs something today to calm her down, and though she's not really ill, there's a little yellow pill." Novelist Jacqueline Susann called them *dolls* in her novel *Valley of the Dolls*. Woody Allen gave the drug a cameo role in several of his films, in *Annie Hall*, Diane Keaton memorably crawls on the floor in search of her Valium.

In the 1979 film *Starting Over*, Burt Reynold's character had a panic attack in the furniture department of Bloomingdale's. "Does anyone have a Valium?" his brother called out as Reynolds hyperventilated. Every woman in the store reached into her purse and pulled out a little vial of pills!

For the first time, psychiatrists had a pill that their patients could take without much stigma. Even the normal looking people seemed to benefit from it without becoming zombie like. A whole new culture built up around this pill, preaching it was alright to take a happy pill for the ups and downs of daily life, if prescribed by a physician. Taking a pill to feel normal led to a societal confusion as well, to what indeed was *normal*. What did it mean when people felt more like themselves with the drug than without? Did it mean many people were *deficient* in a chemical and the pill corrected it? By raising these soul-searching questions, Valium even attempted to redefine the human psyche in substantial ways.

At the same time Valium was entering the medicine cabinets of even conservative, middle-class, suburban families, it also was establishing notoriety for ruining lives of the ordinary people as well as the famous. Elizabeth Taylor, Betty Ford and Tammy Faye Bakker admitted their addiction to Valium. The autopsy report of Elvis Presley revealed that he had consumed large amounts of Valium along with other drugs. In Barbara Gordon's memoir, *I'm Dancing as Fast as I Can*, the television producer-author admitted that quitting Valium cold turkey landed her in a mental hospital. She said, "I, an intelligent woman, became a junkie to my doctors." Karen Ann Quinlan, whose chronic vegetative state was debated by the public and court houses, originally lapsed into a coma from a combination of Valium and alcohol. A 1975 *Vogue* story, "Danger Ahead! Valium-The Pill You Love Can Turn on You," warned that the drug could result in a "far worse addiction than heroin." However, Sternbach, the man behind the creation of Valium, defended his creation, asking the public to pay attention to "the suicides that were averted and the marriages that were saved because of this drug."

Whom to Treat?

In the 21st century, even with far less social stigma attached to anxiety meds, public and health experts still struggle to determine whom with anxiety should be treated with medications. National Institute of Mental Health reminds us—occasional anxiety is a normal part of life. You might feel anxious when faced with a problem at work, before taking a test, or making an important decision. It goes on to say—anxiety disorders involve more than temporary worry or fear- the anxiety does not go away and can get worse over time—can interfere with daily activities such as job performance, school work, and relationships.

Headache is not a disease or disorder, only a symptom, however, alright to manage it by taking Tylenol or Motrin. Hardly anyone worries about it! Unfortunately, the powerful reluctance to take a pill for *occasional anxiety* continues. Taking it for feeling anxious when *faced with a problem at work, before taking a test, or making an important decision?* No way! Doc, can I take pill before taking the flight to New York? Well!

For the health providers, the reluctance to prescribe a medication for the subclinical anxiety or a *Mind problem* was not due to their lack of efficacy, but due to the unknown fear of addiction monster. Many physicians would look at those asking for even a few pills of Xanax or Valium through a tinted glass.

Don Harris described how he overcame his problem after making major live changes and penned it in the book, *10 % Happier*. "In 2003, I became depressed—In an act of towering stupidity, I began to self-medicate, dabbling with cocaine and ecstasy—One of the first things I learned when I consulted a shrink after the on-air meltdown was that the probable cause was my well-hidden and well-managed (or so I thought) drug use."

The ABC News correspondent further wrote about his boss and mentor Peter Jennings assigning him to cover *Faith*—"Thus began a strange little odyssey. Leveraging my position as a reporter, I explored everything from mainstream religion to the bizarre fringes of self-help to the nexus of spirituality and neuroscience. The accidental yet enormously helpful end result of all this poking around: I became a reluctant convert to meditation." Harris is a good example, solving a health problem, sometimes may need more than one thing. He accomplished it by giving up his drug habit and practicing meditation.

CHAPTER 8
SWINGING MOODS

"**M**y tides were fluctuating, too—back and forth, back and forth—sometimes so fast they seemed to be spinning. They call this rapid cycling. It's a marvel that a person can appear to be standing still when the mood tides are sloshing back and forth, sometimes sweeping in both directions at once. They call that a mixed state." In 2004, Jane Pauley, the American television anchor and journalist, announced her diagnosis of bipolar disorder.

The presentation of this illness in its extremes could be dramatic, an onlooker without psychological insight would be astounded to watch these spectacular changes, wondering if it was the same person *doing* it all! The *show put on* by an individual with multiple personality disorder in front of an audience or a full-blown panic attack inside a crowded shopping mall would be small compared to the sudden awakening of a melancholic person from deep a slumber to manic frenzy with fire and heat, more of a mind equivalent of a volcanic eruption with sparkles and flashes!

Without treatment, the lives of people with this devastating illness would be an enactment of a comic-tragic opera, the presenting scene depending on which neurotransmitters were playing havoc inside their brain. The comedy part would be hilarious and gregarious, with sexual innuendos and low-grade jokes. The depressive gloom often enacted behind the curtains would be of a person, whose energy drained, leaving him or her with a numb feeling and no motivation, finding life hopeless and hard to put up with.

Rosemary Clooney

The American singer and actress Rosemary Clooney wrote, "Like an atomic bomb, there had been so much compressed into my brain since childhood, I was ready to explode—All the neutrons and protons of life were out of control—In Sao Paulo I hit a new high. The pendulum swung 180 degrees- mania set in—not sleeping—too much to do. San Paulo was exotically exciting and Brazil was gorgeous, fantastically beautiful. I loved it. The concerts were great, and I was enthralled with all the beautiful nightclubs, where good music was always playing. I went to some fantastic parties where the press and photographers had a field day with me. I was witty. The quotes were sensational and I got lot of press coverage."

Patty Duke

In 1982 Patty Duke put on a *performance* in the office of Sid Sheinberg, the president of MCA and one of the most powerful men in the entertainment industry, after she was summoned to his office for her erratic, unruly behavior. Duke described the incident in her book *Call Me Anna*. "Sheinberg wasn't there, so while I waited around I touched everything on his desk, just like a four-year-old, too self-absorbed to be afraid. I liked the Mickey Mouse clock, one of those little Baby Bens, so I picked it up and put it into my pocket. Sheinberg finally came in and he started reading me the riot act. I said, if he didn't like it, he knew what he could do. He said, 'You're gonna have to not talk to me that way,' and I said, 'Who are you, the dean?' Then he said something else that got me very angry and I said, 'Go to hell. I don't have to put up with you. Keep your two grand a week.' And I threw his Mickey Mouse clock at him (he caught it) and left."

Gentle Versions

Both Clooney and Duke suffered from a clinical disorder that was hard to hide, easily bursting out of the personal confines to the work place, neighborhood, streets, ER, and even get the attention of police precinct. Kay Redfield Jamison, the American psychologist wrote about the mood swings, "The fast ideas are far too fast, and there are far too many; overwhelming confusion replaces clarity, humor replaced by fear and concern, you are irritable, angry, frightened, uncontrollable, and enmeshed totally in the blackest caves of the mind." This is a more serious version, however, many get afflicted with its milder versions, not easy to separate the day-to-day *Mind Problems*. Jamison described it, "When you're high it's tremendous. The ideas and feelings are fast and frequent like shooting stars. Shyness goes, the right words and gestures are suddenly there, the power to captivate others a felt certainty. There are interests found in uninteresting people. Sensuality is pervasive and the desire to seduce and be seduced irresistible."

John Ratey in his 1998 book described, *Shadow Syndromes: The Mild Forms of Major Mental Disorders That Sabotage Us,* about those with the docile forms of mood disorders without reaching clinical significance. According to National Comorbidity Survey Replication, almost 40 percent of those with a history of major depression, also had hypomania, not easy to diagnose if the symptoms were mild. If a relationship in doldrums or marriage breaks down, the couple is more likely to blame their lack of chemistry, different value systems and personalities, and less likely to consider the mood changes as the culprit. However, these mood problems can come out as sexual escapades or gambling sprees or substance abuse problems, without holding the banner of a mental disorder. Sometimes, even the marriage counselors may miss out on the underlying issue, since the symptoms are so subtle.

Helpful Clues

Only by keeping a high index of suspicion, the mild versions of mood swings can be identified in a timely manner. The helpful clues are:

- Any mood change, if associated with decreased need for sleep and increase in energy
- If caused by an event or incident, the symptoms were out of proportion to it
- If caused by substance ingestion, the abnormal behavior continued even after the substance was well out of the system
- If it emerged in a family already afflicted with mood changes
- If the mood swing is spontaneous; meaning to feel *natural high*

without a reason
• If it is causing changes in personality, impulsivity and even bringing on creativity

Any clinical depression has the uncanny ability to switch to bipolar disorder; however, the risk is higher under following circumstances:

• If the depression emerged in a family already afflicted with bipolar disorder
• If the first episode had an early onset; at teenage years or early 20s versus much later on
• If the victim had two or more episodes of depression
• It a previous depression was psychotic in nature
• If the depression was associated with hypersomnia
• If the prescribed antidepressant began working faster than the usual 2 to 3 weeks
• If the antidepressant produced more euphoria, more than a simple relief of depression
• If the depression was not responding to the conventional treatment with antidepressants

High U.S. rates

A National Institute of Mental Health (NIMH) study involving eleven nations reported that 4.5 percent of the American population had bipolar disorder, while the international average was only 2.4 percent! The study published in the *Archives of General Psychiatry* also reported that about half of the U.S. cases were the milder forms. Experts found it hard to explain this interesting finding, some speculating that American doctors over diagnosing these conditions, especially with the rapid climb in the U.S. children and adolescents getting this diagnosis. Others wondered if the widespread usage of psychostimulants, prescribed and illegal, making Americans more vulnerable to develop mood swings. Some even conjectured if the American culture of over-achieving and sleep deprived nights increased such risk.

Power of Genetics

Mood disorders are highly genetic, running amok within the families, however, not affecting everyone the same. Some family members may have both the mania and depression, while others get afflicted with the depression alone. In the midst of this utter chaos, some with its milder versions can easily go unnoticed, believing they are normal or only have a *Mind Problem* such as arrogance, misery, vanity or volatility. Some others may get branded as a wife beater, reckless driver, or the one with road rage and so on.

The first genetic study of mood disorders was conducted more than 70 years ago, revealing their high heritability. A longitudinal study led by John Nurnberger from Indiana University School of Medicine and published in the *Archives of General Psychiatry* showed the lifetime prevalence of major mood disorder was 23 percent higher for the children born in families with a history of bipolar disorder. If minor versions were included, these numbers would be even higher.

Nick Craddock and Ian Jones described the bipolar disorder in the Journal of medical genetics as a complex genetic disorder with the lifetime prevalence of 1%, the family, twin, and adoption studies providing robust evidence for a major genetic contribution to risk. The approximate lifetime risk was estimated as monozygotic co-twin 40-70%; first degree relative 5-10% and unrelated person 0.5-1.5%.

At Johns Hopkins University, the researchers interviewed all the first-degree relatives of patients with bipolar I (more severe form) and bipolar II disorder (milder form) and concluded that bipolar II disorder was the most common affective disorder in both family sets. The researchers found that 40% of the first-degree relatives of the bipolar II patients also had bipolar II disorder; 22% of first-degree relatives of the bipolar I patients had bipolar II disorder. However, among the patients with bipolar II, researchers found only one relative with bipolar I disorder. They concluded that bipolar II was the most prevalent diagnosis of relatives in both bipolar I and bipolar II families.

It's Management

In a family with the mental disorders, any newly emerged *Mind Problem* should be considered a part of it, until otherwise ruled out by a professional. The family should not jump the gun, calling the person a drug addict or narcissistic or sociopath, until evaluated to rule out any other underlying psychopathology. In this context, even the post-partum blues and atypical grief reactions can become significant.

Mood swings can be highly sensitive to the sleep deprivation, usage of prescribed and illicit stimulants and even to the therapeutic doses of antidepressants. At times, even simple stress may be enough to start the fireworks of mood swings, if there was enough genetic loading to ignite it. Rarely, they also have the tendency to come out in weird combinations, a sad event precipitating a natural high and a happy event causing depression!

The professional management depends on the symptoms and complications, the medications playing a major role in calming down the mood changes. This day and age, more and more physicians would favor usage of the medications even for mild to moderate mood changes that were well-below the clinical markers, if they causing disruptions to the smooth flow of everyday life. These small ones also have the potential to become full-blown clinical disorders.

The medication management of mood swings can be complicated, since it is a double-headed serpent, suppressing one head can bring out the other head more ferociously. The important points to remember:

- Mood stabilizers, antidepressants and even antipsychotics have a role in the management of bipolar disorder and even in the mild mood swings
- Treatment will vary depending on the phase illness. What worked for mania or hypomania may not work for the depression. What worked for the depression may not work for mania
- The antidepressants and psychostimulants like Ritalin and Adderall have the risk of precipitating mania. If the antidepressants are needed, such risk can be lowered by combining it with mood stabilizers or antipsychotics
- Antipsychotics have the ability to prevent the person coming out of depression. This risk is worse with typical antipsychotics like

Haldol and less likely with atypical antipsychotics
- Mood stabilizers generally have better efficacy against mania and hypomania; some have antidepressant effect as well
- Some mood stabilizers have higher incidence of side-effects and also will need lab workup to find out the blood level as well as any complications. The antipsychotics as well will need lab work to detect any metabolic changes
- Many patients with bipolar disorder would end up with poly-pharmacy, increasing the risk of side-effects and complications. A careful physician should be able to make the medication regimen less complicated.

Lithium

The first mood stabilizer medication that emerged was Lithium and the credit for this serendipitous discovery goes to John Cade who took up a job at Bundoora Repatriation Mental Hospital in Melbourne, Australia after the Second World War. It was at an unused kitchen in Bundoora where he conducted crude experiments with guinea pigs that led to an effective treatment for manic-depressive illness.

Due to the continued lithium concerns in the United States, it was approved by FDA only in 1970. Cade received belated accolades from all over the world and was invited to be a Distinguished Fellow of the American College of Psychiatrists, as well as made Officer of the Order of Australia. Remaining humble about his chance discovery of lithium, he described himself as merely a gold prospector who happened to find a nugget!

Lithium heralded the era of modern psychopharmacology and several other effective medications followed. This natural salt, the discovery of antipsychotic drugs and the emergence of MAOIs and tricyclic antidepressant medications gave the biological psychiatry a strong footing. The arenas where psychiatry practiced began to shift from the secretive, huge brick buildings managed by the States and the psychoanalytic chambers with well-cushioned Freudian couches, to the modern professional buildings adjacent to the general hospitals, and physicians' offices tucked inside shopping malls.

The profound changes brought on to the mental specialty by lithium and its cousin drugs were factual as well as symbolic, almost akin to what happened to Catholicism in the Second Vatican Council held in 1960s, when some of the old Christian dogmas were refined and the mass was celebrated *versus populum*, the priest facing the congregation, even the language of mass, Latin, changing to vernacular languages. Psychiatry decided to say goodbye to its Latin as well, the Freudian language, and instead accepted a new language of the biological psychiatry of chemical imbalances and neurotransmitters.

CHAPTER 9
DREADFUL ENVY

Envy is an overwhelming, negative emotional experience due to one person wanting what another possesses or, even worse, wishing that the other does not have it at all. It is a never ending game in which it impossible to achieve satisfaction at any time, since the primary motive is to outdo or undo the advantages others have. According to Melanie Klein, the Austrian-British psychoanalyst, envy was an innate expression of destructive impulses, present from birth and resistant to change!

"Instead of comparing our lot with that of those who are more fortunate than we are, we should compare it with the lot of the great majority of our fellow men. It then appears that we are among the privileged." These powerful words have an extremely special meaning coming from Helen Keller, the first deaf-blind person who earned a Bachelor of Arts degree. By grit and determination, she overcame the Himalayan odds against her and achieved astounding success in life.

Aesop's Fable

Two neighbors came before Jupiter and prayed him to grant their heart's desire. One was full of avarice and the other eaten up with envy. So to punish them both, Jupiter granted that each might have whatever he wished for himself, but only on condition that his neighbor would have twice as much. The Avaricious man prayed to have a room full of gold. No sooner said than done, but his joy was turned to grief when he found that his neighbor had two rooms full of the precious metal. Then came the turn of the Envious man, who could not bear to think that his neighbor had any joy at all. So he prayed that he might have one of his eyes put out, by which means his companion would become totally blind!

Aesop's Fable brings out the callous and disgusting nature of envy that is readily recognizable and appalling to anyone. However, this filthy state of mind is more likely to exist without being scandalous and repulsive, more as a *Mind Problem*, often hiding as a poisonous snake in a hole, coming out and biting those around from time to time.

Schadenfreude

The German word *Schadenfreude* literally meant harm-joy, defined as pleasure at the misfortune of others. Philosophers and evolutionists have commented on this miserable state from their own perspectives. While Aristotle defined it as the pain caused by the good fortune of others, for Immanuel Kant it was a reluctance to see our own well-being overshadowed by another's.

British philosopher Bertrand Russell described envy as one of the most potent causes of unhappiness and going into its dynamics he added, "Beggars do not envy millionaires, though, of course, they will envy other beggars who are more successful." Baltasar Gracian, the Spanish philosopher pointed out, "The envious die not once, but as oft as the envied win applause." However, the evolutionary view has tried to explain envy as a biological drive that enhanced an individual's survival, involving a motive to outdo or undo the advantages others have!

Being too docile to find a place in the hierarchy of mental disorders, envy is more of a significant *Mind Problem*. The syndicated columnist Charley Reese stressed its self-destructive danger saying, "If malice or envy were tangible and had a shape, it would be the shape of a boomerang." For Spanish novelist Carlos Ruiz Zafon, envy was the religion of mediocre, "It comforts them, it soothes their worries, and finally it rots their souls, allowing them to justify their meanness and their greed until they believe these to be virtues." Marilyn Monroe, due to her upbringing and subsequent fame saw it in different way and said, "Success makes so many people hate you. I wish it wasn't that way. It would be wonderful to enjoy success without seeing envy in the eyes of those around you."

Religious Views

It has to be very easy for the moral theorists and religious pundits to condemn envy, since there is absolutely nothing positive in this contrite behavior. The first tale on morality in Bible is the downfall of Adam and Eve brought on by an envious serpent. The second story is of Cain and Abel, the brothers who competed for God's attention and approval. Finding God favoring Abel, driven by envy Cain kills his brother. Envy is designated as one of the seven deadly sins of the Catholic Church.

Hinduism considers envy as a disastrous emotion. "One who does not envy but is a compassionate friend to all—such a devotee is very dear to me," said Lord Krishna in Bhagavad Gita. This concept is put forth in the epic Mahabharata, wherein Duryodhana launches the Kurukshetra war out of envy of the perceived prosperity of his cousins. He is known to have remarked: "Father, the prosperity of the Pandavas (cousins) is burning me deeply. I cannot eat, sleep or live in the knowledge that they are better off than me."

In Islam, envy is an impurity of the heart and can destroy one's good deed. Muhammad said, "Do not envy each other, do not hate each other, do not oppose each other, and do not cut relations, rather be servants of Allah as brothers—" A Muslim may wish for himself a blessing like that which someone else has, without wanting it to be taken away from the other person. Buddhism uses the term *irshya*, the state of mind in which one highly agitated to obtain wealth and honor for oneself, but unable to bear the excellence of others. Buddha emphasized—Do not overrate what you have received, nor envy others. He who envies others does not obtain peace of mind.

Jealousy

Jealousy is a close companion of envy that has a special inclination to wreck marriages and family relationships. According to the American moral and political philosopher John Rawls, if envy was the wish to get what one did not have, jealousy involved the wish to keep what one had. William Penn, the philosopher, articulated the pain of jealousy saying, "The jealous are troublesome to others, but a torment to themselves." The American country music artist Gary Allan pointed out the insatiability of jealousy by saying, "You can be the moon and still be jealous of the stars."

Jealousy often involves the suspicion or anger about a perceived betrayal, fear of losing an important person to another. In a nationwide survey, marriage counsellors reported that jealousy was a problem for one-third of all couples who sought counseling, and in some marriages, this spousal jealousy dominated the whole relationship. Those burdened by it often try to control their partners by fabricating lies, manipulating events and even making threats. They themselves may be constantly ruminating about it, day and night, losing sleep and appetite and creating health problems. The victims, suffocated by the constant jealous behavior live with ambiguous feelings, at times even afraid for their own safety. Many may entertain the 'D' word inside their private heads, however afraid to spell it out fearing the consequences.

Steven Stosny, the author and founder of CompassionPower said the formula of this kind of jealousy was, "An insecure person times an insecure relationship." The jealousy by men may be more intense and get more publicity, however, in surveys women reported it more often than men. In one study, these numbers were 63 percent and 27 percent, respectively. It was very much possible men reported this less often, considering even admitting such, a sign of weakness!

The jealous person either did not develop a heathy basic trust or it got eroded by later life experiences. For those already with suspicious tendencies, this stress would be enough to tilt the balance, making this person paranoid, driven to check a partner's undergarments for stain, bed sheets for foreign hair, scrutinize credit card bills to validate their suspicion, showing up at home unexpectedly and so on.

Redemption

Acknowledging envy or jealousy as a problem was the first step towards redemption, not an easy task for a proud person, as revealing it might feel shameful, like belittling oneself. Well, that can be the starting point, the agony of mind providing better motivation. Therese J. Borchard, Associate Editor of World of Psychology, offers ways to overcome jealousy and envy in different spheres in life:

- Get more information
- Compliment her/him
- Do one thing better than him/her
- Put the ladle (and the running shoes) away. One person's success doesn't rob another of success
- Learn from her/him. Your enemy-friend is doing something right, if she/he has your attention. There is a reason you are threatened
- Go to the core. Believe in yourself
- Find yourself. Give yourself a pep talk. Pump yourself up
- Do your best. The ultimate weapon against jealousy and envy is simply to do your best

In spousal jealousy, there may have been already silent treatments, lack of intimacy and dwindling down quality times. Some jealous people may be constantly struggling with their feelings of anger and guilt, a home-made bomb ready to explode with huge repercussions. If this true and unable to communicate with spouse, these hoarded emotions keep on building, such a person should seek out a responsible family member or a trusted friend to talk to. Any time physical threats are made in a relationship, it is highly important to involve others, even legal authorities as appropriate.

Those with good insight may be able to reveal their innermost fears to their spouse, using this as a good time to analyze the entire relationship, seeking professional help, if a decent accord cannot not be reached. It is possible for underlying emotional problems such as obsessive-compulsive disorder and even a paranoid disorder to trigger and maintain jealousy. The healthy spouse too has to carry-out a soul-search to find out if any missing trigger points, and also reveal their side of the story to partner filled with self-doubts. Many relationships are saved by the couples on their own or with the family help, and if not through the professional intervention.

CHAPTER 10
TENUOUS SUSPICIONS

I n 1930, the British philosopher Bertrand Russell put forward his commonsense ideas to attain happiness. "All that I claim for the recipes offered to the reader is that they are such as are confirmed by my own experience and observation, and that they have increased my own happiness whenever I have acted in accordance with them." In the book *The Conquest of Happiness* he described four general maxims in search for happiness.

- Remember that your motives are not always as altruistic as they seem to yourself
- Don't overestimate your own merits
- Don't expect others to take as much interest in you as you do yourself
- Don't imagine that most people give enough thought to you to have any special desire to persecute you

The philosopher's maxim on the persecution would be useful if the fear came from a fully rational mind. However, if the exaggerated fears emerged from the deep unconscious, no intellectual white-washing would make them any easier to bear. With no trust in any fiber in their body, those with deep suspicious tendencies live in a confused, unnatural world and struggle in their personal lives and relationships.

Basic Trust

The basic trust is a powerful human instinct with vast social implications, brought on by both biological and psychological factors, profoundly influencing the newborn from the very beginning. The little one with zero surviving skills instinctively seeks out help, and how it is received will play a significant role in the development of the basic trust. If there is continued physical and emotional negligence, it is likely to leave un-healing wounds, bleeding an entire life. While Freud got fixated on the psychosexual development of the child, the psychoanalyst Erik Erikson emphasized on the psychosocial growth. Freud's *oral* stage was the *trust versus mistrust* stage for Erikson, in which the children learnt to trust or mistrust their caregivers. According to him, the children who did not receive adequate care were the prime candidates to develop mistrust in life. As grownups, they continue to live in their muddled cocoon and the kind of things the healthy-minded people take it for granted without wasting even a fraction of a second, become hard for them to handle.

Genetics vs Environment

A team of researchers at the University of London examined nearly 5,000 pairs of 16-year-old twins to figure it out and published their findings in *JAMA Psychiatry*. Their conclusion, 50 percent of paranoia was hereditary, while the other 50 percent influenced by a combination of environmental factors. The genetic penetrance can be varied within the same family, some developing the delusional paranoia of severe intensity, while others coming out with a tenuous paranoia, more of a *Mind problem*. Those with it may look and behave normal most of the time, however, their suspicious attitude can have a pervasive effect not only on their daily living, but also on the life decisions of vital importance. It would not be easy for them to enter into close relationships since they could not trust anyone completely and even if they did, they were more likely make the other person's life miserable through argumentativeness, combative attitude, unwarranted complaining or hostile aloofness. Such behaviors have the potential to elicit a hostile response in others, which makes them more convinced of their original beliefs! It is hard to deal with them rationally due to their secretive ways, unnecessary rage and constant watching for hidden meanings in gestures and conversations. A 2004 published study by Combs DR and Penn DL on the role of subclinical paranoia on social perception and behavior revealed that those with mild paranoia had greater depression, social anxiety, self-consciousness and lower self-esteem.

Insane

Are the paranoid people insane? Insanity includes a wide spectrum of irrational behaviors that deviate from the prevailing social norms, a concept well recognized throughout the human history. It is very much possible for the paranoia to become intense and delusional, crossing the threshold to insanity. In primitive cultures, witch doctors or shamans applied magic, herbal mixtures, or folk medicine to get rid of the evil spirits from the insane people. Skulls unearthed from the early days had holes bored using flint tools, possibly in some cases as treatment to let the devil out. Ancient Israelis believed insanity was caused by angry God as the punishment for their sins. For the Greeks, it was the result of imbalance of bodily humors, Hippocrates concluding that excess of black bile resulted in the derangement of mind. In the modern thinking, insanity is often equated with schizophrenia, paranoia being a major part of this illness.

"Imagine a thousand more such daily intrusions in your life, every hour and minute of every day, and you can grasp the source of this paranoia, this anger that could consume me at any moment if I lost control." Jack Henry Abbott was a criminal released from prison in 1981, while serving sentences for forgery, manslaughter and bank robbery, after gaining praise for his writing. Six weeks after his release, he fatally stabbed a man during an altercation and was convicted of manslaughter and returned to prison, where he committed suicide.

Some historians have wondered if Soviet leader Joseph Stalin and Nazi leader Adolf Hitler were paranoid. Stalin did not trust anyone around him, even his closest supporters and this trait played a large part in his lack of mercy and brutal ways, killing millions. Hitler has been given several mental titles, such as psychopath, megalomaniac, paranoid personality disorder, the most pronounced through all of these was his paranoid traits. History has recorded the misadventures caused by the paranoid leaders and the misfortunes inflicted by them on innocent humanity.

PPD

When a person has suspicious attitude in a variety of contexts and they are present since early adulthood, such clinical condition is called Paranoid Personality Disorder. The DSM 5 listed their troublesome behaviors:

- Suspects without sufficient basis that others are exploiting, harming or deceiving
- Preoccupied with unjustified doubts about the loyalty or trust-worthiness of friends or associates
- Reluctant to confide in others
- Reads hidden demeaning or threatening meanings into benign remarks or events
- Persistently bears grudges
- Perceives attacks on character or reputation that are not apparent to others
- Recurrent suspicions without justification regarding fidelity of spouse or sexual partner

After listing the troublesome behaviors of PPD, DSM made the stipulation that at least four of them had to present to diagnose this personality disorder. Nothing wrong with this approach, however, it was ignoring the vast number of people who had one or two or three of the symptoms. Can they be listed, those with only a *Mind Problem*.

Suspicions

Call it doubt, distrust, skepticism or inkling, the suspicion is the vague notion of something, often of a negative nature. It can very well be based on reality or entirely fictional. Terry Stafford brought forth this concept in the song *Suspicion*, the words reflected on something that may have happened in many relationships:

Every time you kiss me, I'm still not certain that you love me
Ev'ry time you hold me, I'm still not certain that you care

Though you keep on saying—You really, really, really love me
Do you speak the same words—To someone else when I'm not there?
Suspicion torments my heart, Suspicion keeps us apart
Suspicion why torture me
Ev'ry time you call me -And tell me we should meet tomorrow
I can't help but think that—You're meeting someone else tonight

Unpleasant suspicion comes in different forms, many with its soft versions may be able to live quietly without showing it out to the public, however, a stressful situation or eroding relationship have the ability to bring it out into open. However, those who live in close quarters with them likely to get a glimpse of it from time to time, through unexpected outbursts and irrational behaviors. Marriage counselors meet these individuals amidst relationship meltdowns and family service professionals get involved, when there are outrageous parental behaviors.

In an April 2006 issue of Health.am W.W. Meissner described the paranoid traits that were *muted* and *subtle*. They were continuous, with a more normal range of personality characteristics and functioning, and often difficult to evaluate for this reason. The "soft signs" of paranoia are listed as:

- Centrality—often these people believe that they are somehow the center of other people's interest or attention
- A facade of self-sufficiency—which may represent an attempt to defend against underlying narcissistic vulnerability
- Concern over autonomy—this is fragile and easily threatened
- Blaming—a tendency to blame others for any personal failures, shortcomings or disappointments
- Feelings of inadequacy
- Concerns over power and powerlessness

Management

The suspicious person often ends up living in their own imaginary cocoon, distancing others who can be of help. Many of them may never get proper treatment, unless caught up in a legal tangle brought on by their paranoid behavior or a trusting family member was finally able to convince them to receive help. Even the professional management can get complicated since they need a physician or therapist they trust. Those who did not respond to the psychological treatments or the ill effects of paranoia was significant, may need medication treatment. The most commonly used group of meds are the antipsychotics.

When the first antipsychotic emerged in early 1950s, its impact on the biology of psychosis was profound. It provided a refreshing look at the theory of dopamine, a prominent ingredient of the chemical *soup* of the brain, and convincing evidence that the mayhem of the mind was not caused by poor mothering or societal neglect, but by chemical turmoil inside the brain. One more piece was found in solving the puzzle of mental illness.

The new chemical stopped the demonic voices and irrational beliefs of psychotic patients, and instead filled their minds with hope and ambition. The demand for the brain butchers to perform lobotomies diminished and the shock men gave the new pill a chance to work before resorting to their treatment. The social changes that followed the introduction of this medication were dramatic. The ancient, outdated State hospitals of brick buildings with undersized windows were forced to open their powerful steel doors and release thousands of inmates, who were no longer certified a danger to themselves and others.

The antipsychotic medications have a role in the management of soft paranoias as well. However, the medication may not be the answer for all the paranoid people. Some may benefit even from scenic manipulation. Scenic manipulation! It helped a Second World War veteran who did not receive relief to his distressing symptoms from the pills.

Change in Scenery

Samuel, a veteran who lived in Illinois close to St Louis developed a late onset paranoid disorder, becoming concerned about the police harassment. He spotted police cars outside his apartment that followed him whenever and wherever he travelled by the bus. He was certain his phone was tapped and even changed the number, however it did not stop it. He changed his apartment three times to rid himself of the police presence, once even moving to Missouri; however the harassment continued. He went to the police station and begged them to stop the game they played on him. Feeling sorry for him, they advised him to go to the hospital. Finally, he did and got admitted for an evaluation. Upon arrival in the unit, he demanded an explanation to what went on by asking—Doctor, I paid my dues for my country. Why are they doing this to me, now? No explanations would satisfy him and no medication alleviate his fears. He had three hospitalizations within a short period of time.

The veteran was an only child and his mother passed away when he was young. He remained single all his life and took care of his father until the old man died. The police harassment began immediately after the father's departure. By nature, he was a loner who kept to himself and rarely talked even to the neighbors. Father's death shut him off from all the forms of meaningful communication.

Samuel always felt safe inside the VA hospital, even the hospital security in the uniform did not bother him. At the third admission, an idea was presented to him about living in a group home with other veterans, rather than by himself. He was reluctant at first, afraid he would he would lose his privacy, however, slowly the idea sunk in. Before he left for the veteran's home, he revealed that his deceased father was policeman!

Samuel did not have any more admissions due to his imaginary police harassment. The only son of the police man lived rest of his life among others who served the country during peaceful times and gruesome wars. The improvement in him was entirely due to the change in scenery.

CHAPTER 11
UNDUE SHYNESS

Timid, insecure, or self-conscious, whatever term used, shyness is a universal phenomenon with negative connotations and implications. However, in certain cultures, it is sanctioned and even admired, the parents bragging about their shy child being well-behaved, and the society perceiving shy adults as being thoughtful and intelligent. For those who live in the U.S, the shyness can be a horrible handicap, holding them back the in almost all the spheres in life, creating difficulties in forging relationships and building up a family, make it tough to establish a good career and reach decent financial goals. Shyness was not a part of the American psyche of "rugged individualism, powerful egoism and conquering spirit, no abode for weaklings in this land of the free and home of the brave."

Emma Stone, the talented actresses was *immobilized* by it and late-night television legend Johnny Carson could not perform as well, off stage due to it. Al Pacino revealed his first language was shyness, Steve Martin explained how he balanced out his shyness, and Don Rickles told how he became very outgoing to protect his shyness. Jane Austen, the romantic English novelist, exposed her predicament saying, "I never wish to offend, but I am so foolishly shy, that I often seem negligent, when I am only kept back by my natural awkwardness." Daphne du Maurier, the British author and playwright wondered, "—how many people there were in the world who suffered, and continued to suffer, because they could not break out from their own web of shyness and reserve, and in their blindness and folly built up a great distorted wall in front of them that hid the truth."

Timid Child

The excited parents will watch carefully the developmental milestones of their newborn—sucking mother's milk—crying when thirsty—responding to sounds—smiling—enjoys playing peek-a-boo—say 'dada' and 'mama'—waving 'bye-bye'—shows out pleasure in company, and so on. In the midst of all these joyful moments, there may be concerning behaviors sprouting out from the young ones. If the child was shy and quiet, naturally the parents would get concerned. If such behavior was persistent, they would even worry about the little one's future—how much would this affect the child's education and career? Would he (she) have difficulty in finding friends? Would this prevent them from getting married and settle down with own family?

Should they be concerned? After all, these kids have to live in the land of *rugged individualism, powerful egoism and conquering spirit.* Barbara Markway came up with questions for parents to ask themselves to child's reactions to social and performance situations, in a 2013 Psychology Today and suggested to seek help if answered "*yes*" to several of these questions.

- Do your child's reactions interfere with academic/school functioning?
- Do your child's anxiety interfere with making and keeping friends?
- Is your child missing out on fun activities that many children of the same age enjoy and that your child would likely enjoy?
- Do you spend time worrying about your child's shyness?
- Is shyness or social anxiety affecting how you feel about your child, or how your child feels about himself or herself?
- Is your family environment affected by your child's anxiety? Do you tiptoe around, trying not to set him or her off?

Commonality

A team of researchers at the National Institute of Mental Health studied 10,000 kids between 13 and 18 years of age for shyness and published the findings in the journal *Pediatrics*. In that large sample, about half of the kids described themselves as shy. 50% of girls and 43% of boys reported they were "*somewhat*" or "*very*" shy, and 12.4% met the diagnostic criteria for the Social Anxiety Disorder (SAD).

A recently reviewed article that Bernardo Carducci co-wrote with Zimbardo confirmed this high incidence of shyness. The authors reiterated that even though only 15 to 20 percent of the shy people actually fitted the stereotype of the ill-at-ease person, all suffered internally. According to University of Pittsburgh psychologist Paul Pilkonis, the other 80 to 85 percent are privately shy, though their shyness leaves no behavioral traces, "Even though these people do fairly well socially, they have a lot of negative self-thought going on in their heads."

Shyness being only a *Mind problem* was likely to be ignored by most people, considering it as only a part of their everyday living. It was not unusual even for the health professionals to downplay it, since it was not a clinical disorder. However, even these subtle ones have the penetrating ability to impact the individual negatively, in their thoughts and actions. It is possible for some people with this limitation to become impulsive, taking quick decisions to look bold in front of others! This is more likely to happen when the shy person imbibes alcohol or pills in their attempt to subdue their unpleasant companion.

In a shyness survey by the *Psychology Today* 82% reported shyness as an undesirable experience, the majority attributing it to external factors beyond their control. Only 24% attributed it to internal factors within their control. The majority of those with shyness experienced it daily, most commonly around strangers, persons of opposite sex in a group or even one-on-one.

Nature vs Nurture

Did the young ones born shy or become shy from their life experiences? The experts who looked into this concluded that the heredity played a larger role in shyness than in other personality traits. Developmental psychologist Jerome Kagan and colleagues at Harvard University were able to identify shyness in young infants before the environmental conditions made an impact. In their longitudinal study of four-month olds, 400 infants were subjected to selected stimuli to measure their shyness, and they also were brought back at a later age for further study. From their extended observation, the team concluded that about 20 percent of infants displayed such nervous-system reactivity and would grow distressed when faced with the unfamiliar people, objects, and events. Harvard psychiatrist Carl Schwartz found the staying power of shyness into adolescence by interviewing 13 and 14 year olds who were identified as inhibited at two or three years of age and found they tended to smile less, made fewer spontaneous comments and reported more shyness than those identified as uninhibited children.

In a major twin study, the researchers at the University of Colorado and Pennsylvania State University observed fraternal and identical twins in their homes and in the laboratory, when they were 14 and 20 months old. Their data showed that the genetics contributed substantially to the babies' tendency to cling to their mothers, cry or exhibit other shy behavior when encountering a stranger, new toys and other novelties and concluded that the genetics constituted roughly half of the foundation of shyness.

Is there a gene responsible for shyness? While comedian Jonathan Katz joked about it saying, "Scientists have found the gene for shyness. They would have found it years ago, but it was hiding behind a couple of other genes," the scientists have been actually searching for it for a while. Suspicion landed on serotonin when in 1996 geneticist Dean Hamer of the National Institutes of Health and colleagues reported that they found an association between the serotonin transporter gene and neuroticism, a complex of behaviors that included depression, low self-confidence and shyness around strangers.

It's Physiology

The Harvard study as well as the one by Nathan Fox of the University of Maryland revealed the key physiological differences between the shy and non-shy children. When the shy ones met a stranger or encountered other unfamiliar situations, their hearts beat faster and stronger, their muscles tensed, and they secreted higher levels of stress hormones than the children who were not shy. Also, the shy children had stronger brain wave activity on the right side of the frontal lobe, while the non-shy children showed just the opposite. Other studies have shown higher-than-normal fetal heart rates due to external stimuli that continued after birth in the shy children. The experts attributed this variation in response threshold to the amygdala, the brain structure linked to expression of fear and anxiety, its hyper-sensitivity *educating* some children to avoid the stressful situations.

SAD

Social scientists may have discussed about shyness for centuries, however, its severe form emerged as a psychiatric disorder only in 1980, a diagnostic title bestowed on someone with marked fear or anxiety in social situations, which exposed to possible scrutiny by others. Social Anxiety Disorder (SAD) or Social Phobia became a common diagnosis for the youngsters and adults, men and women, in the hands of mental health providers. Its occurrence in United States has been estimated to be about 7% during a 12-month period, higher rates recorded in the females. According to the Diagnostic Manual the median age of onset for SAD was 13 years, about 75% coming out of the hiding between the ages of 8 and 15.

Even today, there are those who wonder if the psychiatric experts are stretching something a normal part of human life like shyness to a dreadful condition as SAD. Another concern was whether the shyness and the social anxiety differed qualitatively or quantitatively. The general evidence was for both conditions to be significantly different, while many people with SAD shy, shyness was not a pre-requisite for SAD. Only about one half of those diagnosed with SAD reported being shy.

Introversion

This behavior trait has often been equated with introspection, contemplation, timidity and even shyness. Susan Cain, the author of the book *Quiet: The Power of Introverts in a World That Can't Stop Talking,* disagrees and points out the difference between shyness and introversion. "Shyness is inherently uncomfortable; introversion is not. The traits do overlap, though psychologists debate to what degree." The author, a self-described introvert, argue that present Western culture misjudge the capabilities of introverted people, leading to unused talent and energy. She even felt the society was biased against them, some placing this condition, somewhere between a disappointment and pathology.

Typically viewed on a continuum, the terms *introversion* and *extraversion* were popularized by Carl Jung, extraversion manifested in outgoing, talkative, energetic behavior, whereas introversion was more reserved and solitary behavior. The introverts did not necessarily fear the social encounters like the shy people and enjoyed more solitary activities such as reading, writing, using computers, hiking and fishing.

Karin Slaughter, the American crime writer whose first novel, *Blindsighted,* became an international success, admitted, "I am extremely introverted. I used to think it was shyness, but I got over that, so it must be door no. 2. It's still hard for me to be away from home much, and I have to make sure I get lots of time alone in my room when I'm touring."

Cost of Shyness

The article Bernardo Carducci co-wrote with Zimbardo was titled, *Cost of Shyness* and it went on to say—the costs—take on different forms over a lifetime—a shy childhood may be a series of lost opportunities—shy kids also have to endure teasing and peer rejection—make prime targets for bullies—shyness predisposes to loneliness—shyness brings with it a potential for abusing alcohol and drugs as social lubricants—and loss of time. Shy people waste time deliberating and hesitating in social situations that others can pull off in an instant—shy people may focus all their thoughts and feelings on future consequences.

Stanford University psychologist Philip Zimbardo wrote in 1975 *Psychology Today* in an article titled, *The Social Disease Called Shyness* that "Their mild-mannered exterior conceals roiling turmoil inside—they are excessively self-conscious, constantly sizing themselves up negatively, and overwhelmingly preoccupied with what others think of them." The painful consequences of shyness were not only internal and social, but it also could result in cognitive impairment in which shyness prevented clear thinking in the presence of others, with tendency to freeze up in conversations.

Comorbidity

For most people with shyness, it smoothly flowed forward as a docile river, only occasionally becoming turbulent, well-visible to the onlookers. All the studies on comorbidity is geared to SAD, however, such findings can be inferred to shyness, to a lesser extent. SAD is notoriously linked to the depressive and anxiety disorders, as if an opportunistic infection waiting to get in at a weak moment, causing more havoc. These connections are so strong, it even raises the possibility of a common genetic thread connecting all the three disorders. Also visible in association with SAD are phobias, body dysmorphic disorder and avoidant personality disorders. It should not be surprising various phobias are associated with SAD, since its other name is Social Phobia.

It is easier to figure out the emergence of substance abuse in shyness and SAD, since the distressing anxiety in social situations can be curtailed to some extent by substance usage. No wonder, the social lubricant alcohol was at top of the list, followed by usage of anxiety medications. According to a report published in June 2010 Psychological Medicine, 28% of men and women who were diagnosed with SAD met the criteria for lifetime prevalence of alcohol use disorder.

Managing it

Being an ingrained part of personality, the shyness manifested with varied intensity and its subtle forms would hardly concern the parents. There was no reason to worry about, if the child went in hiding when a stranger showed up in the house and showed up later hesitantly, to draw attention to themselves. These children came out of this interesting phase in life fast without any scars. The same was true with the subtle shyness as well.

Many with even the significant shyness become better as they get older, learning new adaptive skills on their own or with the help of parents and the encouragement of teachers. There are several social skills they can learn from others, in a gradual fashion—sharing the toy with younger brother—saying hi to the next door girl—making a phone call to a classmate—inviting a friend for birthday and so on. Some children learn to overcome their limitation simply be talking. One did not have to be Johnny Carson or Al Pacino, Steve Martin or Don Rickles to accomplish this! Even many adults too, handle their shyness with the goal of preventing anxiety, by changing their life style and learning new coping skills. The modern world provides a lot more opportunities for shy people to work in solitary environments or even from home.

If the child's shyness was problematic, it would come to open more clearly by the school entrance, receiving the immediate attention of teachers. It would stand out prominently in the classrooms, the child scared of doing or saying anything out of fear of negative reactions, being laughed at and made fun of. Good teachers handle it well, asking questions to them in a less direct manner, gently encouraging them to speak up in the class, and to make friends with other children. It is important to keep in mind, shy children have the same intensive desire to be heard like all other children, only the fear holds them back. The initial focus always should be the educational remedial measures.

Unremitting shyness causing life problems may be inching towards SAD and needs professional help. The treatment of choice would be cognitive-behavioral therapy (CBT) and may be medications. Medicines are well-accepted in the management of SAD and they may have role even in significant shyness. These include antidepressants including Monoamine oxidase inhibitors (MAOIs), Benzodiazepines and Beta-blockers. If responding well, the impact would be on the anxiety associated with shyness, allowing the child to regain the losses brought on by the shyness.

CHAPTER 12
OBNOXIOUS GREED

"**T**he point is, ladies and gentleman, that greed—for lack of a better word—is good. Greed is right. Greed works. Greed clarifies, cuts through, and captures the essence of the evolutionary spirit. Greed, in all of its forms—greed for life, for money, for love, knowledge—has marked the upward surge of mankind. And greed—you mark my words—will not only save Teldar Paper, but that other malfunctioning corporation called the USA. Thank you very much." With these words, Michael Douglas concluded the speech he delivered to shareholders of the company in the 1987 movie *Wall Street*.

Greed, the inordinate desire to acquire or possess more than one needs, whether for the money, fame or power, mostly takes pleasure to be seated on a well-cushioned pedestal, however, enjoys to exhibit its thunder and glitter to the outsiders from time to time. It creeps in slowly, eroding the human morality, by tightening up its hold through one's teenage years. While it may be childhood poverty which pushes one person to greediness out of the fear of losing it all one day, another person born in lavishness can still driven into it, wanting to imbibe more. Experts believe that many children who were neither impoverished nor wealthy still developed greedy behaviors because of the parental negligence in setting limits and failing to teach them the importance of delayed gratification.

German social psychologist and humanistic philosopher Erich Fromm described it as, "a bottomless pit, which exhausts the person in an endless effort to satisfy the need without ever reaching satisfaction." It is hard for such people to attain the sustained happiness, their unpleasant behavior manifesting as a significant *Mind Problem*, and creating conflicts within self and with others. Since this viper is tightly clung to one's personality, the bearer of it would have a hard time recognizing it as a problem. With their limited insight and also because the greed at times produces positive returns, such people are likely to lead their lives without too much concern about their behavior, until an unexpected, devastating event takes place as the result of it.

Man with Magic Cup

The first short story written by Khaled Hosseini, author of the best-seller *The Kite Runner,* was a dark little tale about a man who found a magic cup and learned that if he wept into the cup, his tears turned into pearls. But even though he had always been poor, he was a happy man and rarely shed a tear. So he found ways to make himself sad so that his tears could make him rich. As the pearls piled up, so did his greed grow. The story ended with the man sitting on a mountain of pearls, knife in hand, weeping helplessly into the cup with his beloved wife's slain body in his arms!

King of the Mountains

Each year in the month of July, a 21-day, 2200-mile, gruesome and demanding bicycling event, Tour de France, takes place in France. The riders from all over the world pass through the mountain chains of the Pyrenees and Alps, and finish on the Champs-Élysées in Paris for a chance to wear the prestigious yellow jersey. This once-in-a-lifetime victory was repeated *seven* times consecutively by American Lance Armstrong.

The tough man told the world, "If you worried about falling off the bike, you'd never get on." He also reminded, "Pain is temporary. It may last a minute, or an hour, or a day, or a year, but eventually it will subside and something else will take its place. If I quit, however, it lasts forever." It was not too long after Armstrong's final victory, the doping controversy surfaced. It was investigated and ultimately culminated in the United States Anti-Doping Agency disqualifying him from all his victories since August 1, 1998, including his seven consecutive Tour de France victories, and a lifetime ban from competing in professional sports. Humbled, still holding onto his grandiosity, he told others, "Nobody needs to cry for me. I'm going to be great." He reminded the world, "The riskiest thing you can do is get greedy. There comes a point in every man's life when he has to say: Enough is enough."

Smaller Versions

In the long human history, it is not just the professional glories tarnished by this monster, it has also brought down vast empires, destroyed rich monarchies, eroded long-standing dynasties, and publically humiliated popular politicians. More like a *Mind Problem*, even its mild versions can bring on bad surprises and interrupt the normal rhythm of human life. The school kid cheating in an exam to do better than a friend, the person spreading false rumors about a fellow employee to get a promotion, the son badly investing his elderly mother's savings in a risky money scheme to make a quick buck are such examples.

Once greed becomes the driving force of daily existence and everything revolves around it with intense obsession, it is hard for such a person to attain happiness in meaningful ways. It involves so much self-centeredness, making it difficult to keep up with nurturing relationships and friendships. It is not easy to be in love with the money and a life partner intensely at the same time and many marriages have been destroyed due to it. With their tunnel vision, the greedy people can only see their unquenchable desires, everything else becomes secondary to it, and they keep on living denying the truth, getting defensive and upset if someone points it out.

Greed needs an object to ignite it and that's how others see and hear about it. That object may be a huge bank balance to brag about, well-doing stocks on Wall Street, an expensive sports car in the driveway, a big house in a prestigious neighborhood and so on, the never-ending desires brooding more. Since the process was less important and fulfilling to such people, even when what acquired lost its glamor, the greedy person may not realize it and keep on looking for more flimsy adventures, thinking it would bring in true happiness.

Religious Views

Religious traditions clearly see greed as the desire and attempt to acquire the material goods. Jesus warned his followers against the seductiveness of wealth, telling it was easier for a camel to go through the eye of a needle than for a rich man to enter heaven. In the Book of Luke, Jesus also warned, "Be on your guard against all kinds of greed; for one's life does not consist in abundance of possessions." Christian ethical education in the fourth century AD identified greed as one of the deadly sins. St. Paul, the founder of Christian theology wrote, "Love of money is the root of all evil."

The Jewish take on greed is complicated by the public perception of this community that has gone through tremendous adversities throughout history. In many minds, Shakespeare's Shylock character stood out in their memory and parallel with it went the success of Jews, especially in business and banking. A 2008 Pew Forum Institute study found that Jews were the nation's wealthiest religious group, with 46 percent earning $100,000 or more a year, compared with 18 percent of the overall population. The most recent Forbes list of the 400 richest Americans included nearly 100 Jewish billionaires! The distorted public view of the rich Jews was not helped by the financial criminals such as Bernie Madoff and Jack Abramoff.

Islam shuns greed, seeing it as an offence that brings on abjectness and sin—Greed is the key to trouble and carries man to hardship—It causes him to commit sin—sign of the wretched. In Hindu theology, *Arishadvarga* are the six passions of mind or desire: kama (lust), krodha (anger), lobh (greed), moha (attachment), mada or ahankar (pride) and matsarya (jealousy); the negative characteristics of which prevented man from attaining moksha or salvation.

Psychoanalytic Views

Sigmund Freud argued that greed was natural, the man born greedy. Melanie Klein, a follower of Freud also saw greed as part of human nature, though, she traced it back to the death drive, saying the human beings were unavoidably self-destructive and projected that onto the outside world in the form of insatiable acquisitiveness, envy and hate. Heinz Kohut, the Austrian-born American psychoanalyst who radically reinterpreted Freud, took a rather different view, saying the man born well and it was the environment that corrupted him. Psychoanalyst Richard Geist saw greed as compensation for the emptiness resulting from the feeling one did not get enough love or affirmation in life. When this happens, "They grow up to be the type of people who try to force others into meeting their needs. In the process, these individuals become aggressive, manipulative, enraged. And when their grandiosity becomes pathological, you get greed."

Socrates to Greenspan

Socrates pointed out, "He who is not contented with what he has, would not be contented with what he would like to have." William Shakespeare in *Macbeth* brought out the danger of greed, "This avarice strikes deeper, grows with more pernicious root." Mahatma Gandhi educated the humanity, "Earth provides enough to satisfy every man's needs, but not every man's greed."

German philosopher Friedrich Engels believed that from the first day to this, sheer greed was the driving spirit of civilization. Actor Larry Hagman identified the late Seventies and Eighties as the age of American greed and explained why Dallas hit a chord then. "Here you have this unapologetic character who is mean and nasty and ruthless and does it all with an evil grin. I think people related to JR back then because we all have someone we know exactly like him. Everyone in the world knows a JR." Unfortunately, there are JRs living in every community, most of them the mini-versions, carrying out havoc in their lives and of those associated with them. The deep penetration of greed into the American psyche made the former Federal Reserve Board chairman Alan Greenspan tell Congress that the *infectious greed* contaminated U.S. business.

Why is it greed pops up so often among humans? Did it begin from day one in life, indulging in the *pleasure principle*, sucking mother's milk, some finding it hard to give it up even after grown up? Possessions can bring in pleasure and easily become addictive, needing more and more, mistakenly associating this pleasure with true happiness. Evolutionary psychologists view greed as a biological drive, giving an advantage to those who acquire more in life, enabling them to build up higher social status and making them more attractive to the opposite sex. If this was true, then what greedy people doing was just the opposite. The research found that money-minded people had less happy marriages compared to the couple not preoccupied with wealth. Jason Carroll, a professor at Brigham University, pointed out this effect held true across all levels of income. It was even worse if both the partners were highly money minded. Some miss out on the point, what really needed to make life happy is a healthy amount of ambition that can become a good motivator in life's endeavors, allowing the person to attain noble heights, without tainted by greediness.

Greed is also present across the animal kingdom. The inhabitants of certain islands of the Indian Ocean found an interesting method to catch monkeys. After drilling a small hole into a coconut, they empty it out and stuff some of the monkeys' favorite food inside. Later, attracted by the smell of this food, a monkey squeezes its hand through the hole, grabs food, and then discovers it cannot pull its enlarged fist out of the hole. Why doesn't it just drop the food and try again? The greedy monkey doesn't want to let go off the food! While the bewildered animal is trying to figure out how to remove the coconut from its hand, it is quickly captured with a net. The moral of this is like the monkey, we can easily become the prisoners of our own greed, the slaves of our own addictions. We have to let it go.

Chuang Tzu, the influential Chinese philosopher who lived around the 4th century BC wrote, "He who considers wealth a good thing can never bear to give up his income. He who considers eminence a good thing can never bear to give up his fame. He who has a taste for power can never bear to hand over authority to others. Holding tight to these things, such men shiver with fear; should they let them go, they would pine in sorrow."

Managing It

Lucky are those who only have a healthy ambition and not get bitten by the greedy bug. The first step in recovery is its acknowledgment, without getting upset even if someone else points it out. The next step is to recognize that greediness can affect every facet of daily life, may come out even in a normal conversation with life partner or while educating own child on the moral values. Since the greedy achievements have to be validated, it may make surprise entry while trying to get a promotion or discussing with the fellow employees on the value of money or raising money for church or discussing or showing off the new house to the family and friends.

It is not easy to change a trait that has been ingrained to one's personality. At times, each greedy element needs to be chiseled out, one by one, by resisting the temptation to compare with others, and trying to genuinely rejoice in their successes. It is important to suppress the desire to show off, instead spending more time in more endurable value systems.

According to Adam Smith, 18th century Scottish moral philosopher and pioneer of political economy, the greed can be harnessed to serve social end, spurring entrepreneurial innovation and leading to broad prosperity. John D. Rockefeller, described as the most cut-throat greedy man as well as the greatest philanthropist, was once asked "How much do you need to have enough?" He replied, probably in jest, "Just a little bit more." This pious, religious man gave away money more than anyone did, to calm down his greediness and justify the vicious tactics he used to build up his fortune.

Comedian Richard Pryor, afflicted with Multiple Sclerosis (MS), for him those two letters stood for 'More Shit," was voted in 2004 as the No. 1 on Comedy Central's list of the 100 Greatest Stand-ups of All Time. Before he died the following year, he admitted that, "There was a time in my life when I thought I had everything—millions of dollars, mansions, cars, nice clothes, beautiful women, and every other materialistic thing you can imagine. Now I struggle for peace."

If the greed continued without fading, hurting self and others, and forcing the person to struggle for peace, it should be subjected to psychotherapy. The intense greed also should be assessed as an OCD trait and some of them may respond to the medication treatment.

CHAPTER 13
GROSS ARROGANCE

Arrogance, a close cousin of greed comes from the thinking—I am better, smarter and more important than other people. It takes the form of an offensive display of one's superiority or self-importance, and with no nobility in this behavior, it brings on misery to those with it. Leo Tolstoy wrote "An arrogant person considers himself perfect. This is the chief harm of arrogance. It interferes with a person's main task in life—becoming a better person." Desmond Tutu, the South African social rights activist and Nobel Peace Prize recipient said, "Arrogance really comes from insecurity, and in the end our feeling that we are bigger than others is really the flip side of our feeling that we are smaller than others."

Arrogant people are looked down by a rational society, even when they try to act to be normal and friendly. It is easy to detect arrogance even behind a smiling face! In relationships, such people are kept at a distance by those who want to avoid their irritating sting. If already living in close quarters, some would suffer in silence, others seek relief by breaking up the relationship. Even when well-qualified, they can be disliked by the potential recruiters and bosses, and denied jobs and promotions. They may even be fired due to their gross behavior for making others around them to feel resentment and anger, thus contaminating the work place.

Golden Swans

There is a folktale about a group of arrogant, golden swans who mistreated a homeless bird. It goes this way: In a faraway kingdom, there was a river, which was home to many golden swans and they spent most of their time on the banks of the river. Every six months, the swans would leave a golden feather as a fee for using the lake. The soldiers of the kingdom would collect the feathers and deposit them in the royal treasury.

One day, a homeless bird saw the river. "The water in this river seems so cool and soothing. I will make my home here," thought the bird. As soon as this bird settled down near the river, the golden swans noticed her. They came shouting. "This river belongs to us. We pay a golden feather to the King to use this river. You cannot live here."

"I am homeless, brothers. I too will pay the rent. Please give me shelter," the bird pleaded.

"How will you pay the rent? You do not have golden feathers," said the swans laughing. They further added, "Stop dreaming and leave at once." The humble bird pleaded many times. But the arrogant swans drove the bird away.

"I will teach them a lesson!" Decided the humiliated bird. She went to the King and said, "O King! The swans in your river are impolite and unkind. I begged for shelter but they said that they had purchased the river with golden feathers."

The King was angry with the arrogant swans for having insulted the homeless bird. He ordered his soldiers to bring the arrogant swans to his court. He asked them, "Do you think the royal treasury depends upon your golden feathers? You cannot decide who lives by the river. Leave the river at once or you all will be beheaded," shouted the King. The swans shivered with fear on hearing the King and flew away never to return. The homeless bird built her home near the river and also gave shelter to all other birds in the river.

Overconfidence

"You are as young as your self-confidence, as old as your fears; as young as your hope, as old as your despair," wrote Samuel Ullman, the American poet. Confidence is an admirable quality, however too much of it can come off as cocky and lead to unwanted obstacles. Christie Hartman, an internationally recognized dating expert and behavioral scientist wrote, "Arrogance is being full of yourself, feeling you're always right, and believing your accomplishments or abilities make you better than other people. People often believe arrogance is excessive confidence, but it's really a lack of confidence. Arrogant people are insecure, and often repel others."

Parents would want their children to be confident, however, advise not to be overconfident in what they did, whether it was an exam or sports or essay competition. Is overconfidence really that bad? Can it be a good thing under any circumstances? Will such a mindset boost the resolve of the individual, to get the task done better?

Psychologists have observed that people routinely overestimate their abilities. They are mystified why overconfidence remains a key human trait despite thousands of years of natural selection, which typically weeds out the harmful traits over generations. Dominic Johnson, an evolutionary biologist at the University of Edinburgh in Scotland, studied this phenomenon and published the findings in the journal *Nature*. "There hasn't been a good explanation for why we are overconfident, and this new model offers a kind of evolutionary logic for that. It's unlikely to be an accident—we're perhaps overconfident for a good reason."

Johnson with James Fowler of the University of California, San Diego, developed a model using evolutionary game theory to explore how the individuals with different strategies performed in competition with each other. Using computer simulations, they showed that a false sense of optimism, whether when deciding to go to war or investing in a new stock, could often improve the chances of winning. They concluded that overconfidence paid off when there was uncertainty about an opponents' real strengths, and when the benefits of the prize at stake was sufficiently larger than the costs.

Angry Mood

If arrogance was an insulting way of thinking oneself superior to others, then anger was the strong feeling of annoyance, displeasure or hostility brought on by it. If arrogance was the thorny mountain with snakes and spiders, then anger was the crater that fumed often and occasionally busted out with red, boiling lava, burning its surroundings.

Anger is an emotion characterized by antagonism toward someone or something one felt done wrong deliberately. It is the first psychological response when a wrong-doing perceived and emerges in a wide range of intensity, from irritation and frustration to outright rage and violence. The experts view anger as a primal and natural emotion experienced by virtually everyone and may have functional value for survival, mobilizing personal resources to the maximum. They consider the appropriate anger giving the person a way to express the negative feelings, motivating to find solutions to problems, and to stand up for themselves and fight for their rights. Most tennis enthlasis's would argue that the anger and temper tantrums displayed on the tennis court by John McEnroe or Jimmy Connors or Ili Nastase did not affect the quality of their game!

Raymond Novaco of the University of California Irvine stratified anger into cognitive (appraisal), somatic-affective (tension and agitation) and behavioral (withdrawal and antagonism). Psychologists recognize mainly two types of anger, the *Hasty and Sudden* one, which is primitive and connected to the impulse of self-preservation and something humans shared with rest of the animal kingdom and the *Settled and Deliberate* one, called dispositional, related more to character traits than to instincts or cognition and manifested as irritability and sullenness.

Angry Brain

Did an angry, untrained brain deliberately make the mind go crazy by setting off uncontrolled fireworks? Is there at least a primitive part of the brain beyond full control capable of generating the impulsive angers, as of snarling wolfs, growling tigers and roaring lions? The role of human brain in producing anger can be vastly more than we think, however, the good news is our minds have substantial control too. The physical brain is not the absolute commanding officer of those with a healthy mind. However, we need to be careful and listen to what Will Rogers said, "Letting the cat out of the bag is a whole lot easier than putting it back in." Many with outrageous anger brought on by an unhealthy brain, more of a *Mind Problem*, find it hard to take it back once let it out.

Scientists have found activity in different parts of the brain associated with anger, angry rumination and aggressive personality. A functional MRI study done by Denson TF and group, and published in the 2004 *Journal of Cognitive Neurosciences* showed that the activities in dorsal anterior cingulate cortex and medial prefrontal cortex were positively related to the self-reported feelings of anger and rumination. The increased activation observed in hippocampus and insula following the provocation also predicted subsequent self-reported rumination.

Douglas Fields, an internationally recognized neurobiologist and an authority on brain and cellular mechanisms of memory spent years trying to understand the biological basis of rage that led him to conclude, our culture's understanding of the problem was based on erroneous assumption that rage attacks were the product of morally or mentally defective individuals. For him it was simply a capacity everyone possessed and in his 2016 book, *Why We Snap: Understanding the Rage Circuit in Your Brain*, he wrote that we could not fully control once engaged and to emphasize his point, he brought out stories of otherwise rational people with no history of violence or mental illness suddenly snapping in a domestic dispute, an altercation with police, or road rage attack. However, an interesting finding was, essentially the same pathway in the brain that resulted in a violent outburst could also enable us to act heroically and altruistically before the willful part of brain knew what we were doing!

Angry Nation

An NBC News/Survey Monkey/Esquire Online Poll conducted in November 2015 among a national sample of 3,257 adults showed half of all Americans were angrier than the previous year! People were deeply upset about injustice and inequality, marginalization and disenfranchisement and about what *they* doing to us, and this anger showed no sign of abating. Is this translating to more violence in the streets and political rallies? There are political experts who believe that President Donald Trump understood this anger well and tapped into it to win the election.

Among Afro-Americans, 70 percent expressed anger about the way they were treated by the society. 48 percent of American women felt the same way and even 21 percent of white men said they angry too, as how they were treated. More than half of those polled reported angry episodes at least once a day. The national anger permeated through all spheres of American life, among various income groups, the angriest were those in the middle-class.

Philosophical Views

Aristotle considered that anger or wrath was a natural outburst of self-defense in situations where people felt wronged, and ascribed some value to anger that arose from perceived injustice, because of its usefulness in preventing injustice. He also said—anybody can become angry and that is easy—but to be angry with the right person and to the right degree and at the right time and for the right purpose and in the right way—that is not within everybody's power.

Other philosophers have acknowledged the need to control anger starting in childhood, since the young brains are more malleable. Seneca took a more cautious view saying, this education of the young ones should not blunt their spirits, nor they humiliated or treated severely; at the same time they not be pampered and their requests not be granted when they angry. Saint Thomas Aquinas was of the opinion, "He that is angry without cause, shall be in danger; but he that is angry with cause, shall not be in danger; for without anger, teaching will be useless, judgments unstable, crimes unchecked. Therefore, to be angry is not always an evil."

Its Dangers

The medical science has clearly proved the dangers of persistent anger, corroding human health. Katherine Kam, a freelance journalist quoted a report in WebMD Magazine in which the researchers found that otherwise healthy people who often angry or hostile were 19 percent more likely than calmer people to get heart disease. Another study found there was a three times higher risk of having a stroke from a blood clot to the brain or bleeding within the brain during the two hours after an angry outburst! For people with an aneurysm in one of the brain's arteries, there was a six times higher risk of rupturing it following an angry outburst!

Harvard University scientists have found that persistent anger weakens the immune system, increasing the risk for infections. The study of 670 men for eight years using a hostility scale scoring method to measure anger levels, and assessing any changes in their lung function, found that the men with the highest hostility ratings had significantly worse lung capacity which increased their risk of respiratory problems. The researchers theorized that an uptick in the stress hormones associated with feelings of anger created inflammation in the airways. A University of Michigan study done over a 17-year period found shortened life span in those stressed out and angry.

It may be easier to measure the impact of anger on physical health, however, it is much harder to quantify its ill-effects on personal well-being, mental health and relationships. How many road rages, divorces, and loss of jobs are brought on by it! With no desire to confront such individuals, the vast majority of people would rather avoid them, rather than put up with them. Whatever explanations offered by the angry person and the sincere apologies that followed each time would not be enough to calm down the nerves in a relationship. Rational and irrational fears are likely to engulf those living in close proximity, worrying about their health and wellbeing, and at times even about their own safety.

Diagnostic Evolution

Sigmund Freud emphasized on the importance of letting the anger out and his colleagues agreed with it—the repressed fury builds up and festers, much like steam in a pressure cooker, to the point that it causes psychological conditions like hysteria or trip-wired aggression. Josef Breuer, the Austrian physician developed cathartic treatment using hypnosis to help his patients with hysteria to bring it out and find relief!

Even with the robust emergence of biological psychiatry and the rapid decline of psychoanalytic hold, the profession is only hesitantly threading into the area of anger, a common

Mind Problem. The first edition of Diagnostic Manual (DSM-I) that came out in 1951 allowed its entry referring to as *passive-aggressive personality* type, characterized by a persistent reaction to frustration, and generally excitable, aggressive, and over-responsive to the environmental pressures.

The DSM-II that emerged in 1968 called it as explosive personality disorder, a behavior pattern characterized by gross outbursts of rage or of verbal or physical aggressiveness, strikingly different from the person's usual behavior. Intermittent Explosive Disorder (IED) made its entry in 1980 through the DSM-III, and received promotion to the clinical hierarchy. It described someone with several discrete episodes of loss of control of aggressive impulses resulting in serious assault or destruction of property and the behavior was grossly out of proportion to any precipitating psychosocial stressor.

DSM-III-R published in 1987 expanded the list of exclusions and noted the prevalence was very rare. The DSM-IV that came out in 1994 deleted the exclusions of generalized impulsiveness or aggressiveness and amended the prevalence from *very rare* to *rare*. There were experts who disagreed with rarity of this disorder and in 2006 Kessler and group reported a lifetime prevalence of 7.3%. Approximately one person in fourteen! DSM-5 emerged in 2013 moved away from several episodes of serious assaults or serious destruction of property to diagnose IED to recurrent behavioral outbursts representing a failure to control aggressive impulses as manifested by either verbal aggression or physical aggression occurring twice weekly, on average, for a period of 3 months, or three serious behavioral outbursts occurring within a 12-month period. The latest DSM of 947 pages has made vast improvements, however, is still struggling with the concept of anger.

IED

This acronym stands not only for *improvised explosive devices* that have killed and maimed thousands on war fronts, but also for *Intermittent Explosive Disorder*, in which the magnitude premeditated aggression was grossly out of proportion to the provocation. It can be confined to temper tantrums, ranting and ravings and outrageous tirades, however, it often gets well-beyond to physical aggression, animal cruelty and property destruction, placing huge red flags in front of family life and job places. It is possible for its milder forms, more of a *Mind Problem* to survive longer, until an unfortunate situation lands them in big trouble.

According to a 2006 Harvard study, 10 million men in the United States suffer from IED. "We never thought we'd find something this big," said Ronald Kesssler, PhD, the lead study author. "People think their anger isn't a big problem. But there are very serious ripple effects. IED suffers are also more likely to be divorced, they have worse jobs than others with the same education, and they have fewer friends." The researchers estimated that only half as many women suffered from IED.

Anger Management

Most situational angers subside with time, if the communication channels are kept open. However, if persistent or suppressed anger are not friendly to human health. It did not mean just letting it out would always dissipate this horrible feeling. Sometimes, other strategies are needed, like talking about it with others, a trusted family member or a friend. Some let it out by putting their angry feelings to writing. This technique can work even if the object of anger deceased—the son writing to an alcoholic mother who passed away, forgiving her for the horrible things she did to him—the daughter writing to stepfather who was no more, to come in terms with her anger due his abuse.

It is a well-known fact, those who can express themselves verbally about their anger are less likely to act upon it. The other way round, those with poor communication skills are more likely to get frustrated while facing stressful situations and act out. As per skills-deficit model, if poor social skills rendered a person incapable of expressing anger in an appropriate manner, social skills training should be considered for those with this deficiency. There are experts who believe that one major reason for men get angry and violent more often than women is due to their inability to express the anger appropriately

Mayo Clinic Staff came up with following anger management tips:

- Think before you speak
- Once you're calm, express your anger
- Get some exercise
- Take a timeout
- Identify possible solutions

- Stick with 'I' statements
- Don't hold a grudge
- Use humor to release tension
- Practice relaxation skills
- Know when to seek help.

Buddha and Disciple

Time can become the healer, as it has been for many human pains. Buddha taught his disciple a lesson on this profound truth, when he was walking from one town to another and happened to pass a lake. He told the disciple, "I am thirsty. Do get me some water from that lake there." The disciple walked up to the lake and noticed right at that moment, a bullock cart started crossing through it, turning the water very muddy.

The disciple thought, "How can I give this muddy water to Buddha to drink!" So he came back and told the master, "The water in there is very muddy. I don't think it is fit to drink." After about a half an hour, again Buddha asked the disciple to go back to the lake and get him some water to drink. He obediently went back to the lake, but this time, too, found that the lake was muddy. He returned and informed Buddha about the same.

After sometime, again Buddha asked him to go back. The disciple reached the lake to find it absolutely clean and clear with pure water. The mud had settled down and the water above it looked fit for drinking. So he collected some water in a pot and brought it to Buddha. Buddha looked at the water and then he looked up at the disciple and said, "See what you did to make the water clean. You waited long and the mud settled down on its own and you got clear water. Your mind is also like that. When it is disturbed, just let it be. Give it a little time. It will settle down on its own. You don't have to put in any effort to calm it down. It will happen. It is effortless." Buddha also pointed out, "You will not be punished for your anger; you will be punished by your anger."

Internal Dialogue

Some people recover from their anger by self-cognitive manipulation, engaging in an internal dialogue to bring in positive results. For
example, in a situation an employee felt tremendous anger towards
the boss over a remark he made in front of other employees—the inner dialogue can be, if appropriate—*He is a good man. He hired me
when I was jobless for a year. He is paying me good, and gave me a bonus
for Christmas. Maybe it was not what he said, others laughing made it
worse. Let it go.* The anger dissipates. Maybe it came back while driving home; again, use the same strategy. Pangs of anger and repeated
inner dialogue. The dialogue will get easier with experience. Road rage!
*How can this fellow cut me off? Let me go after him. Hold it. Why should
I belittle myself, responding to his antisocial behavior? Is he trying to make
me feel inferior by showing off his Porsche? Let it go.* A wife yelling at her
husband who just came home tired after a long day's work; his first
reaction to yell back at her. The inner dialogue should begin immediately—*Maybe she had a hard day at work. Maybe the children gave her a
tough time. Let it go.*

For those who felt the internal dialogue was not to their style, another strategy was to replace the angry thoughts with continuous repetition of a *mantra* word or a phrase, such as *God help me, God is great,*
it did not matter, or *my dear wife I love you,* which may work if she was
the target. Keep in mind what Mark Twain said, "Anger is an acid that
can do more harm to the vessel in which it is stored than to anything
on which it is poured."

Some people help themselves with their deep convictions. Booker
T. Washington, the African-American educator expressed it this way,
"I shall allow no man to belittle my soul by making me hate him."
American televangelist Joel Osteen Joel Scott Osteen preached, "Every
day we have plenty of opportunities to get angry, stressed or offended.
But what you're doing when you indulge these negative emotions is
giving something outside yourself power over your happiness. You can
choose to not let little things upset you." American philosopher Wayne
Dyer found a cure for anger, "It is impossible to be angry and laugh at
the same time. Anger and laughter are mutually exclusive and you have
the power to choose either."

Any anger, if cannot be resolved in amicable ways and taking a toll on a person's health, personal and social life has to be managed professionally through psychotherapy and attending anger management classes. Psychotropic medications have a definite role in subduing uncontrollable anger that not responding to psychological treatments. This is even more important in those with IED. Some with this disorder associated with head injury or seizures can become candidates for anti-seizure medications.

CHAPTER 14
GLOOMY LAZINESS

"I like the word *indolence*. It makes my laziness seem classy,"
so said the British moral philosopher Bernard Williams. The
word is derived from Latin *indolentia* which means *without
pain* or *without taking trouble*. May be this indolence is more like the
idleness, romanticized and epitomized by Italian expression *dolce far
niente*—it is sweet to do nothing. Many people would consider the
weekend a time to idle after working five, gruesome days and the same
attitude taken to a higher level while vacationing once or twice a year—
a time to put behind all the stresses from their job.

Dr. Neel Burton pointed out in his book, *Heaven and Hell: The
psychology of Emotions,* to be idle was not to be doing anything; yes, it
can be because of laziness, but also because one did not have anything
to do or temporarily unable to do it, or perhaps already done it and
resting or recuperating. The author quoted the examples of Lord Melbourne, Queen Victoria's favorite prime minister, extolling the virtues
of *masterful inactivity* and Jack Welch, the former chairman and CEO
of General Electric who spent an hour a day in what he called *looking
out of the window time.*

Unlike idleness, the more commonly used term *laziness* is viewed
pejoratively by the modern societies, and those with this unpleasant
behavior are bestowed some unpleasant titles: loser, idler, loafer, slack-
er, slob, couch potato, freeloader, good-for-nothing fellow and so on.
It is the disinclination to activity or exertion despite having the ability
to act or exert oneself and if sustained becomes an integral part of their
daily life, preventing them from attaining their full potential. Filled in
with low self-esteem as well, this life style forces them to live unhap-
pily, having difficulties to build up good relationships and become a
responsible member of society. The passivity of this life style can fill up
the mind with negative thoughts, further dulling the lazy person, also
leading to unhealthy behaviors such as smoking, drugging, alcohol usage and excessive eating with unnecessary weight gain.

Lincoln's Letter

On January 2, 1851, a decade before he won the presidency, 42-year-old Abraham Lincoln scolded his step-brother, one year his junior, "Your request for eighty dollars, I do not think it best to comply with now. At the various times when I have helped you a little, you have said to me, 'We can get along very well now,' but in a very short time I find you in the same difficulty again. Now this can only happen by some defect in your conduct. What that defect is, I think I know. You are not lazy, and still you are an idler. I doubt whether since I saw you, you have done a good whole day's work, in any one day. You do not very much dislike to work and still you do not work much, merely because it does not seem to you that you could get much for it. This habit of uselessly wasting time, is the whole difficulty; and it is vastly important to you, and still more so to your children, that you should break this habit. You say if I furnish you the money you will deed me the land, and if you don't pay the money back, you will deliver possession. Nonsense! If you can't now live with the land, how will you then live without it?"

Lincoln's critique sternness stemmed from his loving concern and aimed to motivate rather than dishearten his step-brother. To incentivize him to work, he made him a bargain —for every dollar John earned by his own labor in the next five months, Lincoln would make a matching gift and thus double his earnings. And yet even so, he admonished John, any financial aid would be lost on him unless he cultivated a healthier relationship with work, money and property.

Is it a Myth?

Laura D. Miller wrote an article in the October 3, 2015 issue of *Psychology Today* titled, *7 Reasons Why Laziness Is a Myth—but here's what may really be holding you back*. After emphasizing laziness is an overused criticism—a character judgment—that does nothing to help us understand why someone doesn't exert the effort to do what they want to do, or are expected to do, the author listed a range of more complicated issues behind it.

• Fear of failure, afraid if they make the effort, their true inadequacy will be revealed and that can be devastating; better, instead, not to try

• Fear of success; worried that they'll succeed in ways potentially threatening to others; so why not avoid a conflict by not moving forward

• Desire for nurture, acting useless as a way of getting others to do things for them; unable to give up on childhood dependency needs as an adult

• Fear of expectations, so set the bar low as a way to prevent others from having high expectations for them

• Passive-aggressive communication, and communicate through laziness to avoid conflicts.

• Need for relaxation, erroneously assuming that they should always be going full steam, and chastise themselves for being lazy when their body and mind shut down in protest

• Depression. Self-loathing for their so-called laziness is common among those suffering from depression.

It's Psychology

Was the laziness a psychiatric disorder to be identified as such in the diagnostic manual or more of a behavior problem in which such a person was a fully willing partner? Could it be a personality trait if the individual was always this way from the younger days? Or, be a significant *Mind Problem* with enough punching power to disrupt the smooth flow of human happiness and bring on misery and pain?

According to Freudian psychoanalysis the pleasure principle is instinctual, seeking pleasure and avoiding pain in order to satisfy the biological and psychological needs. Freud used the idea that the mind sought pleasure and avoided pain in his *Project for a Scientific Psychology* of 1895. In the *Two Principles of Mental Functioning* of 1911, the psychoanalyst spoke for the first time of pleasure and no-pleasure principle. However, this state of no-pleasure did not equate with the laziness.

Dr. Burton commented on the psychology of laziness pointing out, "In most cases, it is deemed painful for such a people to expend effort on long-term goals that do not provide immediate gratification, un-like the self-confident people who are more apt to trust in the success and pay-off of their undertakings and much more likely to overcome their natural laziness." In spite of its significant negative consequences, laziness would not find a place among the psychiatric disorders and most experts would agree with that. However, the American educator and psychologist Leonard Carmichael pointed out, "Laziness is not a word that appears in the table of contents of most technical books on psychology. It is a guilty secret of modern psychology that more is understood about the motivation of thirsty rats and hungry pecking pigeons as they press levers—"

Low-grade Depression?

Depression is a weird clinical disorder, with some universal warn-ing signs, but also having certain symptoms unique to that person. Everyone depressed person would not have crying spells or loss of ap-petite or insomnia. Some would simply be tired, spending long hours in bed, looking like a lazy person, especially if it happened after losing the job, with no motivation to look for a new one or no desire to go back to school after jilted by the girlfriend. Concerns should be raised if the so-called laziness was not lifelong and came on recently after a negative life event and such a risk was higher for those with family his-tory of mood disorders. This behavior can very well present as a *Mind Problem*, mild in nature and with less separation from the person's daily living, leading to misdiagnosis even by the health providers.

Evolutionary View

From the evolutionary point of view, is there any advantage to hu-man beings for being lazy? Is this not a passive behavior brought on by the active participation of such person who is well-cognizant of its perks and drawbacks? Did it evolve from the need of the early humans to conserve energy on the *rainy* days, being laid back when no action required, so the chances of success of a hunting expedition or escaping a natural disaster would be far better? Well, it may have helped the early man who did not have the mind to fabricate any long-term goals, however, in today's world, the evolutionary theory did not make much sense at all. Even their loved ones would look down on such person bundled up in bed half the time, the other half fixated in front of TV screen, with frequent visits to the refrigerator to fill up the stomach.

Religious Views

In Christianity, the term used for laziness is *sloth* with moral and spiritual overtones, one of the seven deadly sins, because it undermined God's plan and invited sin. Bible denounces slothfulness in the Book of Ecclesiastes—By much slothfulness the building decayeth; and through idleness of the hands the house droppeth through. The Arabic term used in Quran for laziness, inactivity and sluggishness is *kasal*, fasting and praying recommended to get rid of it. In Buddhism, the term *kausidya* is commonly translated as laziness or spiritual sloth and defined as clinging to unwholesome activities such as procrastinating and not being enthusiastic about in engaging in activities.

Managing It

Jon Jachimowicz recently wrote an article in the *Huffington Post*, "Laziness Is More Complex than You Think: How a More Nuanced Approach Can Help Us Overcome Laziness When Needed." He admitted he was a lazy student." My father would often say that I lacked *Sitzfleisch*, a German word… referring to the capability of sitting on your behind and getting your work done. When I reached 11th grade, however, everything changed. I met a teacher who visibly cared about his subject, biology, and what he taught actually interested me. Gone were the days of struggling to study…. by the end of 12th grade, my father stopped calling me lazy and proudly announced that I had finally developed *Sitzfleisch*."

Jachimowicz asked himself, "But was it really that simple? Is laziness a trait that one can get rid of over time? The answer, in my opinion, is a resounding—No. To this day, I am still lazy in some situations, but not in others. Laziness, I believe, is not a trait that one has or does not have but is instead a set of states and habits. I think that what we call laziness is actually a blanket term for a wide range of behaviors that have different roots and origins."

The most important aspect in the management of so-called laziness is to identify if any mental depression present, and if so seek professional treatment to redeem from it. In this context, it needs to be kept in mind, the depressions can emerge with varying intensity, in subclinical forms and as Mind Problem, some unfortunate ones suffering from chronic depressions, lasting years. Bipolar depressions are notorious for causing hypersomnia, such a person spending long hours in bed, looking and behaving just like a lazy person.

Once mental depression ruled out, laziness should be identified as a significant *Mind Problem*, loaded with personality traits and the unhealthy habits. Those who accepted it as an unhealthy habit would get a jump-start, compared to those who concluded it was a part of their personality, thus reaching the wrong conclusions: It is part of me—This the way I was born—Nothing can be done about it now, and so on.

As a habit, even if it was long standing, the strategy should be slowly getting rid of the negative behaviors and replacing them with the positive ones, a supportive family atmosphere helpful a great deal in this solo venture. The negativities to get rid of could be smoking, drinking, sleeping too much and overeating, just to name a few. The positive behaviors could include going for walks, eating healthier, getting more involved with the household chores, and so on. The successes, however slow they may be, should be counted by the number of fewer cigarettes smoked, the abstinent days without drinking and the weight lost each week. The positive events should be expanded slowly to more activities. Of course, no plan would work unless the lazy person had the desire to get better.

CHAPTER 15
INDECENT VANITY

Otto Kernberg was 11 years old when his family fled Nazi Germany and immigrated to Chile. In 1961, he came to the United States after studying psychoanalysis at Chilean Psychoanalytic Society and joined the Menninger Foundation in Topeka, Kansas. It was while there, he described in detail his concept of *Narcissistic Personality Structure*, synonymous with Vanity.

Interestingly, there was a time in the human history *vanity* simply meant *futility* and did not have its modern narcissistic connotation. Religions considered it a form self-idolatry and Christianity looked down on *pride* as a deadly sin. Others have used the terms such as self-love, egotism, conceit, snobbery and so on, to describe this psychological problem of those who lived in their own bubble-castle of success, power, brilliance and beauty, suffocating themselves with their grandiosity and annihilating relationships by their self-centered behaviors.

Narcissus

The classic story of Narcissus came from the first century B.C and is recounted in Book III of Ovid's *Metamorphoses*: a young handsome man falls in love with his own reflection in the water. He kneels down to kiss his image, but he can't have the thing he desires, since the image is broken each time he brings his lips to the water. Then, unable to consummate his love, he lays gazing enraptured into the pool, hour after hour without eating and sleeping, and presumably dies. In another version, Narcissus falls into the water when trying to kiss his image and drowns.

Freud, much inspired by the Greek mythology created not only his Oedipus theory of infantile development but also speculated for years about narcissism, and published in 1914 an important paper *On*

Narcissism: An Introduction, in which he defined it as adoration one accorded themselves in light of them being an object of sexual desire. He postulated that all the humans had some level of narcissism throughout their development and differentiated between the primary narcissism, which he considered existed in all human beings, present from birth and focusing externally, and the secondary narcissism that developed when individuals turned this object affection back on themselves.

Kernberg

Kernberg described the *normal adult narcissism*, in which normal self-esteem was based on normal structures of self, the individual introjecting whole representations of objects with stable object relationships, solid moral system, and superego fully developed and individualized. He also described the *normal infantile narcissism* in which the regulation of self-esteem occurred through gratifications related to the age, which included or implied a normal infantile system of values, demands or prohibitions. Setting aside the normal versions, Kernberg identified *pathological narcissism*, as not merely the libidinal investment in the self but in a pathological, underdeveloped structure of the self itself. This defective structure presented defenses against early self and object images, which were either libidinally or aggressively invested. Within this he described three subtypes:

- Regression to the regulation of infantile self-esteem, the ideal ego dominated by infantile pursuits, values and prohibitions. This is the mildest type of narcissistic pathology
- Narcissistic choice of object. This type is more severe than the first one but rarer and in which the representation of the infantile self-projected on an object, then identified through that same object and from regression to normal infantile narcissism

Narcissistic Personality Disorder

DSM5 sets up the nine criteria to diagnose this condition, however, stipulated the presence of at least five of them to make a definite diagnosis. What happens to those who have less than five? Will they be considered as having only a *Mind Problem*? The DSM criteria are:

- Grandiose sense of self-importance
- Preoccupied with fantasies of unlimited success, power, brilliance, beauty, or ideal love
- Believes that he or she is special and unique
- Requires excessive admiration
- Has a sense of entitlement
- Takes advantage of others to achieve own needs
- Lacks empathy
- Envious of others or believes that others are envious of him or her
- Arrogant, haughty behaviors or attitudes

Narcissistic

British essayist and poet T. S. Eliot who passed away in 1965 wrote, "Half the harm that is done in this world is due to people who want to feel important. They don't mean to do harm, but the harm (that they cause) does not interest them. Or they do not see it, or they justify it because they are absorbed in the endless struggle to think well of themselves."

Narcissists can be charming and helpful most of the time, impressing others even in astonishing ways. Such people live in every community as good parents, responsible citizens and have the ability to become the life of a neighborhood party or a leader organizing a church picnic.

However, with less empathy for the fellow human beings and no desire to relate to the feelings of others, they can easily become unpleasant, displaying anger and throwing temper tantrums. The gentle dove can easily become a woodpecker, eating away the precious wood, only caring about the delicious worm to fill their voracious appetite. Those who live in close quarters are likely to witness this irritating behavior as a significant Mind Problem.

The 2006 Psychodynamic Diagnostic Manual pointed out that narcissism exists "along a continuum of severity, from the border with

neurotic personality disorders to the more severely disturbed levels."
Additionally, "Toward the neurotic end, the narcissistic individuals
may be socially appropriate, personally successful, charming and, although somewhat deficient in the capacity for intimacy, reasonably
well adapted to their family circumstances, work, and interests."

Gone with the Wind

More than three decades before Otto Kernberg introduced his
concept of narcissistic personality, American author Margaret Mitchell
presented it through young Scarlett O'Hara, the spoiled daughter of
a well-to-do plantation owner, in *Gone with the Wind*, a story set in
Clayton County, Atlanta, Georgia, during the American Civil War and
Reconstruction. Scarlett used every talent at her disposal to escape her
way out of the poverty in which she found herself deep in. In the film
by the same title, Vivien Leigh played Scarlett and the film begins with
the actress in the middle of all men, basking in their adulation and saying, "Now isn't this better than sitting at a table? A girl hasn't got but
two sides to her at the table."

Scarlett had to be the center of attention. Often, she was seductive
or provocative, using her appearance to draw attention to herself. Her
emotional display was dramatic, intense and shifted rapidly. She was
highly suggestable with erratic interpersonal relationships and considered her relationship with the character Ashley more intimate than it
was.

On the Rise?

Convinced that the USA was in decline, some social critics in the
1970s seized on narcissism as the sickness of the age, indicting Americans as greedy, shallow and self-indulgent. The 1978 book *The Culture
of Narcissism: American Life in an Age of Diminishing Expectations* by
Christopher Lasch was a scorching denunciation of what seemed to
him the moral emptiness of life in postwar United States. In the same
year, Richard Dawkin published *The Selfish Gene*, a book proposing the

selfish behavior was genetically determined. Very soon, psychologists Robert Raskin and Calvin Hall came up with a Narcissistic Personality Inventory.

Stinson FS et al in an article published in the Journal of Clinical Psychiatry July 2008 put the prevalence of narcissism 7.7 percent in U.S. men and 4.8 percent in U.S. women. More prevalent among younger adults, the group wondered if it was on the rise as a result of the social and economic conditions that supported more extreme versions of self-focused individualism. However, Elizabeth Lunbeck, a historian of human sciences, specializing in the history of psychoanalysis, psychiatry and psychology, took issue with the concept of a new kind of person being born in our shores, through her 2014 book *The Americanization of Narcissism.*

Narcissistic Injury

The concept of narcissistic injury was brought forth by Sigmund Freud and it is a term used for any threat to a narcissist's outsized ego or self-esteem. *Psychology Today* described it this way, "Someone says or does something that hurts deeply. You feel unseen, betrayed, invalidated or simply criticized. You may feel it's unfair or that you deserve it. Either way, you are having a tough time recovering. It eats at you. The hurts somehow sticks. You feel ashamed that you can't just let it go. Or respond in a healthy way. So you either nurse the wound privately, or you lash back in an over-reaction." Of course, the response to the inflicted narcissistic injury would depend on the severity of psychopathology and what caused the injury.

Narcissistic Rage

This term was coined by Heinz Kohut who wrote the seminal article, "Thoughts on Narcissism and Narcissistic Rage" in 1972. Unlike the mature aggression with built in assertiveness, he emphasized that this rage enfeebled the narcissist and they were left instead prone to oversensitivity to perceived or imagined narcissistic injuries. For him, the narcissistic rage was related to the narcissists' need for total control of their environment including the need for revenge, for righting a wrong, for undoing a hurt by whatever means.

Narcissistic rage can be held tightly inside the chest for long periods with hardly any visible signs, but burst out as a reaction to narcissistic injury, a perceived threat to a person's self-esteem or self-worth. It is provoked by the slightest, real or imagined narcissistic insult, whenever such person feels something to which they are entitled is taken away from them, this may be not being seen, understood or appreciated. The rage impairs their cognition and judgement, making them distort facts and indulge in behaviors such as shouting and aggressive gestures. For any outsider, this rage would appear irrational and greatly out of proportion to the situation that provoked it.

Managing It

Narcissists hardly ever seek out help on their own or for such problem alone, since they have only limited insight to this behavior ingrained to their personality. However, they would have certain doubts about themselves, while facing failures and setbacks or totally unexpected life events—*I am shocked my wife left me! I cannot believe it. I was such a good provider. I gave her an expensive car for her birthday*—Or, after getting fired from a job. *Wow! What happened? I was the best employee. I always came up with new ideas. The hell with them!*

Some may seek help due to narcissistic injury if it led to a mental breakdown, the towering skyscraper crumbling down to the ground of reality. For others, it may be the narcissistic rage landing them in legal problems, as domestic violence or road rage or public disturbance, forcing treatment. Those with a family history of bipolar disorder need to watch out for its atypical and subclinical forms affecting some family members in the form of unhealthy narcissism, presenting more like a *Mind Problem.*

If narcissism was complicated by the substance abuse, its proper management should receive high priority, before venturing into any other treatments. It is not unusual at all for the narcissistic rage to burst out in some people only under the influence of alcohol and drugs. Once this problem was under control, the main form of treatment would be psychotherapy, educating the narcissist to develop better insight into their abnormal behavior. Since more like a *Mind Problem*, ingrained to the personality and with no much separation from everyday functioning, dealing with narcissism would not be an easy task. Sometimes, it would be less strenuous to deal with the complications of this behavior, if already affected relationships or work place performance, than dealing directly with the underlying problem.

The narcissistic person may not have difficulty in finding romantic relationships, the challenge would be in maintaining it. In the 2013 book titled, *Disarming the Narcissist: Surviving and Thriving with the Self-Absorbed,* the author Wendy Behary asks—How do you handle the narcissistic people in your life? "You might interact with them in social or professional settings, and you might even love one—so ignoring them isn't really a practical solution." If in an otherwise good relationship, to generate some empathy for such person, it is important to convince self that the narcissistic ego is in a *pathetic* shape, and it sad and lonely to be in this state of mind. Also, make a list of hot-button issues, learning to anticipate and avoid them, and setting limits when it's time to draw the line on unacceptable behaviors.

Narcissists have great difficulty giving up anything they perceived as their *property*—wife, child, house, car—it doesn't matter. If they lose something and find no way to retrieve it, they are likely to present an ugly part of themselves. The February 07, 2011issue of *Psychology Today* included an article by Dr. Karyl McBride entitled, "Help! I'm Divorcing a Narcist." The author advised—if you marry a narcissist and then divorce that person, the narcissist will not forgive and forget. They do not move on easily. They cling to 'how could you abandon me or do this to me' and the anger lingers for long periods of time, sometimes years and years. She went on to say, "The narcissist makes unrealistic demands, may be emotionally abusive or worse, but will fight to the end to gain revenge or fight in the interest of own needs. That person will never get over or forget that you filed for divorce or abandoned him/her, and will continue to make life difficult for you and the children."

McBride added a pessimistic view of severe narcissm, "To imagine that one could process through an amicable divorce with a narcissist and stay friends and co-parent in a reasonable manner was not realistic. They do things like excessively disparage the other parent, resort to making up unfair and untrue allegations, and do not want to financially support the children because that somehow means to them that they are giving money to their ex-spouse. Their entitlement needs get in the way of fairly dividing property and money and in the end they do not think of what is best for the child or children. They think about what is best for them!"

The infamous incident involving O.J. Simpson, his wife and her friend made some mental health experts to speculate if O.J has a narcissistic personality disorder. According to Patricia Saunders, Metropolitan Center for Mental Health in New York, "O.J. is almost a textbook definition of what psychologists call a narcissistic personality. He seems very deficient in terms of a conscience and a capacity to empathize with other people. The hallmark is someone who fails to show empathy for other individuals, even the people he allegedly cares about, and of course a person who acts without a conscience."

CHAPTER 16
EXCESSIVE ODDNESS

Unorthodox behaviors, typically perceived as unusual or unnecessary are considered eccentric and those who consistently displayed them are labeled eccentrics. These behaviors did not have to be bizarre or creepy of an intense nature to cause disruptions in human life, even their mild versions that appear as *Mind Problem* have the potential to bring on misery and discomfort.

Eccentricity has several diagnostic fathers, the most well-known is the Obsessive-Compulsive Disorder (OCD). It has become one of the best recognized acronyms in mental health, even the teenagers know what those three letters stand for. It can be a very subjective experience and many with it try to hide it in shame. However, if it gains power and becomes outrageous, the victims may even wonder if they are going crazy! Those living in close quarters with such person will get frequent glances to this helpless behavior.

Creativity?

Is there a link between eccentricity and creativity? The answer, some creative people may be eccentric, however, that did not mean all eccentric people necessarily had creativity hidden somewhere in them! Harvard researcher Shelley Carson, the author of *Your Creative Brain: Seven Steps to Maximize Imagination, Productivity and Innovation in Your Life* gave examples of strange beliefs and behaviors of some creative people in the May/June 2011 issue of *Scientific American*—Composer Robert Schumann believed that his musical compositions were dictated to him by Beethoven and other deceased luminaries from their tombs—Charles Dickens was said to have fended off imaginary urchins with his umbrella as he walked the streets of London—Albert Einstein picked up cigarette butts off the street to get tobacco for his pipe—Howard Hughes spent entire days on a chair in the middle of the supposedly germ-free zone of his Beverly Hills Hotel suite.

Howard Hughes

Late in his life, this billionaire developed a reputation of being an eccentric person, several such stories emerged from his hide-outs. One such was he spent *months* in the germ-free zone, ignoring his hygiene, watching movies continuously, writing detailed memos to his aides, urinating in empty bottles and containers, and stacking and re-arranging dozens of Kleenex boxes! He was obsessed about the size of peas, a favorite food of his and used a special fork to sort them by size. With the mortal fear of germs, he also picked up objects with tissues. Weakened by his strange behaviors, the grossly emaciated billionaire died in 1976.

Nikola Tesla

Those with OCD have certain universal symptoms, but also unique ones based on their personality, cultural and moral values. Look at this way, who can imitate Howard Hughes with his own brand of eccentricities? Nikola Tesla, the inventor known for his contributions to the design of modern AC electricity, had his own kind of idiosyncrasies. He was obsessed with the number three or with any number divisible by three! He insisted on estimating the weight of everything he ate and having a stack of three, folded, cloth napkins beside his plate at every meal. He developed the compulsion to walk around a block three times before entering a building and insisted on staying in a hotel room with a number divisible by three. In spite of all these, Tesla continued with his work and on his 75th birthday, *Time* magazine put him on its cover. He lived the last ten years of his life in a suite on the 33rd floor of the Hotel New Yorker; the room number 3327!

OCD Spectrum

There were profound differences in how the obsessions and compulsions affected these two brilliant men. While the six-foot four inches tall Hughes died at age 70 weighing about 95 pounds due to his eccentric eating habits, Tesla died at the age of 86 of heart disease, having had a stellar career even towards the end of his life.

OCD strikes nearly one in 100 men and women in U.S, usually before the age of 20. In about 25 percent of people the onset can be even before the age of 14. It varies person to person, however with certain commonalities. It can be counting numbers inside the head, continuously repeating a prayer, word or phrase, an intense desire to have things orderly and symmetrical and being bothered by asymmetry and disorderliness, being confused about horrific thoughts of harming someone or by intrusive thoughts of a sexual and religious nature, a fear of shouting obscenities or acting inappropriately in front of others, repeated doubts about whether or not the door is locked or stove turned off, fear of germs and anxiety about getting contaminated in a public toilet, by shaking hands or touching objects others have touched and avoiding such situations, washing and cleaning to extreme levels.

OCPD

DSM 5 set up the eight criteria for Obsessive-Compulsive Personality Disorder, stipulating four or more needed to diagnose it, leaving those with anything less than that to the mercy of *Mind Problems*. Some would only have rigidity in thinking and stubbornness and inflexible attitudes about the matters of morality, ethics and values, creating conflicts in relationships and workplace. What if the high morality and values preached by a person got translated to the spousal abuse or excessive punishment to the children, leading to legal problems? What if the preoccupation with details led to inferior job performance and maybe even getting fired? Or the excessively devotion to work to the exclusion of leisure activities and reluctance to delegate work, because of the fear it would not be done correctly, leading to poor health. There may be others who have difficulty discarding worthless objects without any sentimental value, develop miserly money spending style, considering even money as something to be hoarded. It would not be a pleasure to live with a person who is always rigid in their thinking or compulsive with their habits. And, if the relationship already delicate, it would not take much of these to add additional stress in the relationship.

Do you have OCD? When health providers ask this question, they don't have to explain what that means. The most common response would be a smile, followed by statements like—I am a control freak— everything has to be in a certain order—It bothers me if anything is out of place. Some would brag about it as if it was all about punctuality, being organized and keeping the house clean. Some people would add after a pause—you mean the real OCD, like checking the door knob, washing hands, no, I don't have it.

Alison Dotson, author of the book 'Being Me with OCD: How I Learned to Obsess Less and Live My Life', wrote, "Your life becomes consumed with a fear and your preoccupation with getting rid of the fear—it becomes a vicious cycle. It's scary to feel like you can't even control your own thoughts." She went on to describe her own condition, "I started obsessing when I was a child, and I wasn't diagnosed with OCD until I was two months' shy of my 27th birthday. I suffered in silence for years and years because all I knew about OCD was that people wash their hands too much and always check to make sure the stove is off. I would think, what type of person thinks things like this? Even though I knew—or thought I knew—deep down that I was a good person, it certainly didn't feel that way when I couldn't stop obsessing about religion and offending God and illegal or immoral sexual acts."

Family Genetics

Family and twin studies have revealed that OCD has a strong genetic component, and is five times more likely to manifest in first degree relatives. The role of anxiety may be the common thread connecting the family members, however, the clinical presentation may vary from person to person within one family. It can be skin-picking or hair pulling in some, others feeling disgusted with their body appearance or counting habit, or simply worrying to death over trivial things. A study published in the April 2000 issue of journal *Archives of General Psychiatry* by Gerald Nestadt and group of John Hopkins School of Medicine verified the same, but also showed the familial type had an earlier onset. When the age of onset was 5 to 17 years, the occurrence of OCD in relatives was 13.8 percent, but it was 0 percent in patients when the symptoms began between ages 18 to 41!

According to Jeffrey Schwartz, author of the books *Brain Lock* and *The Mind and the Brain,* OCD is caused at a neurological level, due to hyper-connectivity between two brain regions, the orbito-frontal cortex and caudate nucleus, creating a tidal wave of unfounded mortal fear and triggering habitual response as the only way to attain calm. "But the worst part is that, despite recognition that all these thoughts and behaviors are irrational, the OCD sufferer feels driven to obey them, nonetheless."

Shadow Syndromes

John Ratey and Catherine Johnson described in their book the *Shadow Syndromes,* for the obsessive-compulsive symptoms too mild to diagnose as a clinical disorder, and pointed out that those suffering from it, even though functional, often struggled in their life. The authors further asked—What was the difference between someone with OCD and someone with just those traits? Maybe the individual with the trait would check school papers three times before handing them in and take two hours to do a one-hour assignment. But once it was turned in, the worry was over, until the next time!

Many people would consider the shadow symptoms as a part of their daily life and not OCD, since they were well- below the clinical par. Experts disagree. A 2005 article in the *International Journal of Neuroscience* reported that the subclinical symptoms shared common neurobiological substrates with the clinical OCD. Donald W Black and group from Iowa studied the children and adolescents with subclinical OCD and found that the subclinical OCD may herald the onset of clinical OCD in some people, in others it may be an independent condition that did not lead to a full disorder. Their findings were published in the September 2008 issue of *CNS Spectrum.*

David Beckham, the retired English soccer player, admitted he had OCD, saying, "I have to have everything in a straight line, or everything has to be in pairs." Interestingly, he had the reputation for *bending* free-kicks and was named in the FIFA 100 list of the world's greatest living players. Film director David LaChapelle commented on obsession, "You work with people who are obsessive about shopping, obsessive about owning things and buying things, like this purchase is going to make them happy. And you want to say to them, you know, no amount of real estate is gonna fill that void." Barbara Streisand, the singer, said she had been called many names like perfectionist, difficult and obsessive. "I think it takes obsession, takes searching for the details for any artist to be good."

Managing It

When OCD emerged as a shadow syndrome, in the subclinical uniform or as a *Mind Problem*, it was not always easy to decide when to be concerned about it. Even the mental health practioners may have different opinions, since the condition was well-below the clinical spectrum. However, Ratey and Johnson points out, "Ultimately, the question is: why should the person with a very mild disorder accept his problems as simply his lot in life? If it is possible to treat a mild and hidden disorder by means of natural or medical intervention, then it is desirable. Even a mild disorder, given time, can damage a life, can drain away joy and hope."

Some people with worrisome feelings succeed in controlling them by engaging in an inner dialogue or by replacing the distressing thoughts with continuous repetition of a *mantra* word of their own choosing. Maybe those with OCD traits have a distinct advantage in implementing this technique! However, if they are getting out of control and making life miserable, professional help should be sought. It is not unusual for many to seek help, at least initially from a family practitioner or show up in a dermatology or plastic surgery clinic with Body Dysmorphic Disorder, a variant of OCD.

OCD is typically treated with the medication, psychotherapy or a combination of the two. Approved medications include Fluoxetine (Prozac), Paroxetine (Paxil), Sertraline (Zoloft), Clomipramine Anafranil) and Fluvoxamine (Luvox). Psychotherapy can be an effective treatment for adults and children with OCD, research showing *cognitive behavior therapy* and behavior therapy helping to reduce the distressing symptoms. Even the shadow syndromes and the ones like *Mind Problems* should be assessed for treatment if they were disrupting the smooth flow of daily life of the victims and their loved ones. The intrusive procedure Deep Brain Stimulation (DBS) may have a role in those with severe OCD intractable to the conventional treatments.

Guidelines for Family

Barbara Van Noppen and Michele Pato from USC Keck School of Medicine developed guidelines to help the family members who lived with those with OCD.

- Recognize the warning signals and do not dismiss significant behavioral changes as just their personality. These changes can be gradual, but overall different from how the person has generally behaved in the past
- Modify expectations, realizing that change of any kind, even positive change can be experienced by someone with OCD as stressful, and often during these times the symptoms tend to flare up
- Realize that people with OCD get better at different rates and avoid day-to-day comparisons
- Recognize small improvements
- Create a supportive environment
- Set limits and be firm about prior agreements regarding assisting with compulsions, how much time is spent discussing OCD, how much reassurance given, how much the compulsions infringe upon others' lives
- It has become all about the OCD! That should not happen. The understanding should be that OCD is not allowed to run the household. Separate time is important for everyone in the family, not just for the one with OCD
- Support taking medication as prescribed
- Keep communication clear and simple

- Keep your family routine normal
- Be aware of family accommodation behaviors. How about the victim's request to join in a questionable ritual, however, benign in nature. It could become beneficial, but also has the risk of perpetuating problems. If you're unsure, professional help should be sought
- Consider using a family contract with the primary objective to get family members and individuals with OCD to work together to develop realistic plans for managing the symptoms in behavioral terms

Robert Plant, the English musician, said, "I like to comprehend more or less everything around me, apart from the creation of my music. It's an obsessive character trait that's getting worse. I don't switch a light on and off 15 times before I leave the room yet, but something's going wrong." It is important to anyone stressed out or burnt out to ask themselves, if any OCD traits playing any role in it. It did not have to be *switching a light on an off 15 times* to create problems in family and social life and vocational pursuit. Even if mild in nature, a *Mind Problem* disrupting the smooth flow of life professional held should be sought.

CHAPTER 17
REPULSIVE IMPULSIVITY

In the hierarchy of animal kingdom evolved through evolution, the humans have been provided with a vastly superior thinking machine and thus can reap its benefits to the maximum. However, when behaviors emerge from an unhealthy mind or without its full consent, life becomes disruptive, affecting the wellbeing of self and others. In this scenario, impulsivity can step in, making such people act on a whim, with little or no forethought to the consequences. It is akin to rapid gunfire into the dark, not fully knowing the target, resulting in direct and collateral damage.

Impulsivity often emerged from childhood and sensitive parents would take note of the rash behaviors with concern. Initially exhibited within the family walls, it gradually shows off in the neighborhood, and later on sprouts out in the classrooms and school grounds. The teachers pay attention to the child who suddenly stands up even when not called upon or gets restless bothering other children and disrupting the entire class or spills milk in the dining hall as if intentionally or gets into fights over silly reasons. When such behaviors continue and the grades get affected, the parents and teachers are likely to suspect the Attention Deficit Hyperactivity Disorder or ADHD.

Some impetuous youngsters will exhibit their mischief through the harassment of classmates, frequent lying, cruelty to animals and destruction of property, and this may even lead to frequent truancy and running away from home, with total unconcern about their performance at school. Their shallow affect, or lack of empathy, remorse or guilt will highly concern the parents and deeply frustrate the teachers, who will try to modify this Conduct Disorder, not an easy task to do so in those with such antisocial traits.

Mood disorders are well known to bring on impulsive behaviors, can be reckless driving or road rage with legal ramifications, altercations at work with risk of losing the job, buying spree or compulsive gambling or foolish investments inviting financial disaster, sexually irresponsible behaviors straining the family life. Impulsivity can also emerge in several other settings, as part Intellectual Developmental disorder or brain injury and seizures, compulsions of the OCD including skin picking or pulling out of one's hair, binge eating and fire setting, failure to resist to steal objects.

BPD

Borderline Personality Disorder or BPD is a clinical disorder, more common among the females, with a strong association with childhood trauma, and characterized by the frantic efforts to avoid real or imagined abandonment. Moods can alternate between the extremes of idealization and devaluation and they struggle to find their own feelings while going through the emotional roller coasters. They can easily bring out impulsive fireworks, becoming angry and hostile, throwing temper tantrums, being manipulative, playing mean games, rejecting help and biting the hands of those coming to their aid. Still, they have the ability to be benevolent angels on their good days, capable of being charming and kind, complimentary and thankful and even trying to provide certain stability to the life of others. DSM5 described the nine criteria of BPD and stipulated the presence of five or more to make a definite diagnosis, those less than that, ending up with *Mind Disorder*.

Their moods were capable of changing rapidly, calm winds giving no clue to the tornado behind it and blue skies misleading the observer to think whatever ahead could be pleasing and beautiful. The noise and color of their day-to-day behaviors depended on how well or horrible their lives had been going, bewildering the onlookers. Their helplessness and pathetic behaviors, anger and rage would create an armada of emotions in those who watched it, the witnesses usually were the loved ones and the health providers. Some of the irrational behaviors could be intentional and manipulative, while others came out of the deep unconscious mind.

BPD used to be the playground of psychoanalytic-oriented psychiatrists, who got excited witnessing the psychoanalytic principles they learnt played out in abundance in their live patients. It was a learning tool for them, as well as a teaching tool. With the psychoanalysis in decline, only some psychotherapy-oriented psychiatrists continue to cling to it, mesmerized by its colorful psychological pathology. The biological psychiatrists often would look at BPD as incurable disease.

This disorder is often misdiagnosed in clinical settings as PTSD and bipolar, even the health providers playing a role in it. In his book, *Searching for Sanity*, the author presented the story of a 24-year-old bartender who was sexually abused by her grandfather which resulted in several hospitalizations from cutting herself. She claimed she was bestowed with two diagnoses: PTSD by those who had empathy and understanding of her; BPD by those who did not like her impulsivity and repeated admissions.

Those with BPD live in every community, living quietly without much fanfare, however ready to burst out under the least amount of stress. They are well behaved until they foresee a threat, then in their defective minds even the miniscule ones can become huge and formidable enough to totally annihilate them. The flimsy attempts to cover up their fragile egos craving for respect usually lead them to devious acts, easily losing the empathy of others around them. Thus, filled with deep unhappiness, they live miserably.

Lost in Mirror

Richard Moskovits wrote about the borderline predicament in the book, *Lost in the Mirror: An Inside Look at Borderline Personality Disorder*. "To be borderline is to have little sense of who you are or what turns you on. At its extreme, it may mean having to turn to others for cues in order to know when to eat or drink, work or rest, or even laugh or cry. It may mean intensely embracing a person, idea, or thing one day, and having no use at all for it the next. This lack of a constant picture of one's self, one's values, or one's passions is at the heart of the borderline personality-"

"Borderlines create the vicious circles they fear most," wrote the psychologist Theodore Millon. "They become angry and drive the relationship to the breaking point, then switch to a posture of helplessness and contrition, beg for reconciliation. If both parties are equally enmeshed, chaos and conflict become the soul of the relationship."

Christine Ann Lawson, the author of the book *Understanding the Borderline Mother*, pointed out "To stave off the panic associated with the absence of a primary object, borderline patients frequently will impulsively engage in behaviors that numb the panic and establish contact with and control over some new object." This can happen even in those who did not have the full spectrum of BPD, even the bits and pieces of this disorder, more of a mind problem has the power to cause much damage.

Marsha M. Linehan, the creator of Dialectical Behavioral Therapy, compared them to those with third degree burns over 90 percent of their bodies. "Lacking emotional skin, they feel agony at the slightest touch or movement." Kimberlee Roth, author of *Surviving a Borderline Parent*, wrote, "Owing to a poorly defined sense of self, people with BPD rely on others for their feelings of worth and emotional caretaking. So fearful are they of feeling alone that they may act in desperate ways that quite frequently bring about the very abandonment and rejection they're trying to avoid."

One piece of good news! Most BPDs are afraid to die. They are more likely to indulge in suicidal gestures than serious attempts, cutting the wrist very superficially or taking an overdose of only minor consequences. However, once in a while, the *smart* one accidently cuts too deep or takes too much of a dangerous medication.

Genetics

Impulsivity is a complex behavior brought on by genetic and environmental factors. Scientists suspect that certain brain structures including the limbic system, linked to emotions and memory functions, and the frontal lobe, the part of the brain's cortex linked to planning functions and controlling impulses affect the disorder. Hormones associated with violence and aggression, such as testosterone, also can play a role in it. For example, the researchers have suggested that women might be predisposed to less aggressive types of impulse control disorders such as kleptomania or trichotillomania, and men to more violent and aggressive types such as pyromania and intermittent explosive disorder. Research also has shown connections between certain types of seizure disorders and impulsive behaviors.

In the 2014 *Neuroscience and Biobehavioral Reviews*, Amad A and colleagues estimated the heritability of BPD at 40 percent. Other researchers have tried to link chromosomal genetic material and dysfunction in the hypothalamic-pituitary-adrenal axis to this disorder. A number of neuroimaging studies have reported findings of reductions in the regions of the brain involved in the regulation of stress responses and emotion, affecting hippocampus, orbitofrontal cortex, and amygdala, amongst other areas.

Managing it

Even if the impulsivity mild in nature, without any other baggage attached to it, still can be hazardous to health and wellbeing, needing professional intervention. Depending on the severity and negative consequences, this would consist of psychotherapy or medications or the two combined to reap better rewards. Short-term hospitalizations to deal with the crisis situations may be needed for those with impulsive, injurious behaviors directed to self or others. The psychotherapy can be long term or intermittent dealing with each crisis. The goal of medication treatment is to improve the mood and reduce the impulsivity. It is not easy for the patients with impulsivity to find a physician or therapist who empathize with them and put up with their unusual demands. Unlike the old fashioned thinking that impulsivity hard to treat, in modern psychiatry their success is measured by their personal happiness, stability in relationships and ability to hold a job without getting fired. In ADHD, the impulsivity is managed with psychostimulants and in bipolar spectrum disorders, such behaviors, even of mild in nature can improve with the mood stabilizers. Those suffering from IED need to be evaluated neurologically, especially if they have history of head injury or seizure. Some of them can be tamed clinically by taking anticonvulsant medication.

CHAPTER 18
TROUBLESOME LYING

According to the experts everyone lies, some every day, most who do it not even realize they are lying. These are the *white lies* that have no consequences and with no intention to hurt anyone. Some of these are even considered a normal part of social life; complementing grandmother on the dinner she prepared, when in fact it was only so-and-so; telling sister the new dress was the perfect on her, when thoughts in the opposite direction was going through the mind; congratulating son on the excellent game he played, even though he happened to be the worst player on that day. Children lie age-appropriately to cover up something *trivial*, due to the fear of getting into trouble—Mom, I did not spill the milk—Dad, Cathy messed up the room—Grandpa is the one who ate the cake, and so on.

Unlike the benign liars who likely to build up healthy relationships and able to live their lives happily, the troublesome ones keep on hurting others around them and by doing so burn themselves badly. They belong to heterogeneous group, encompassing con artists who take pride in their ability to swindle others, those with Conduct or Antisocial Personality Disorder in which lying becomes one of the dominant belligerent behaviors, pathological liars whom no one in the civilized world can put up with, and Psychopaths and Sociopaths, their stories splashing up in the media, after them carrying out atrocious acts.

The list will also include the politicians who lie through their teeth to build up their resume, holy men who get caught red-handed after indulging in unholy acts and essentially anyone, some doing it in a compulsive way, for many others it become a part of their personality. Patrick Couwenberg, a Los Angeles County Superior Court judge was removed from the bench by the state judicial commission, after willful and prejudicial misconduct, perjuring himself during the state investigation. He had repeatedly lied about being a Caltech graduate, a wounded war veteran and a CIA operative in Laos in the 1960s! The fabricated academic and military experience may have helped his appointment to the bench by the California Governor.

In the country built and flourished on the shoulders of George Washington who said, "I cannot tell a lie" when called out about who chopped down the family cherry tree, and Abraham Lincoln whose nickname was 'Honest Abe,' there were other American Presidents, who succumbed to its temptation. Bill Clinton lied, "I did not have sexual relations with that woman, Miss Lewinsky" and George H.W. Bush said, "Read my lips. No new taxes," however, brought out plenty of taxes.

Clinical Disorders

Troublesome lying often begins to unfold at young age as a part of Conduct Disorder, many parents initially reluctant to brand it significant in their attempt to give their little one, the benefit of doubt. However, the full picture unfolds slowly raising concerns—mom, I did not have anything to do with the school bus vandalized—the person teacher called about bullying was not me, it was my friend John—stealing from grandma, no way I would do it—yes, I kicked the poodle, kept on barking whole night, on and on. By their ability to lie outright and the association with other CD behaviors, this population stands out much different from the benign liars. With the need for immediate gratification and the total disregard for the social norms, they continue with their antisocial behaviors as adults, lying becoming an integral part of it. *He* will not hesitate to fabricate one lie on top of other, unable to pay enough attention to the consequences of getting caught. If caught, so what? *He* will tell another lie to escape from the desperate situation or react with an angry outburst.

Psychopathy/Sociopathy

Robert D. Hare, a researcher in the field of criminal psychology who wrote the 1993 bestseller *Without Conscience: The Disturbing World of the Psychopaths among Us,* described such a person. "He will choose you, disarm you with his words, and control you with his presence. He will delight you with his wit and his plans. He will show you a good time but you will always get the bill. He will smile and deceive you, and he will scare you with his eyes. And when he is through with you, and he will be through with you, he will desert you and take with him your innocence and your pride. You will be left much sadder but not a lot wiser, and for a long time you will wonder what happened and what you did wrong. And if another of his kind comes knocking on your door, will you open it?"

Ted Bundy

He was a pathological liar, however, it paled compared to the brutal killings he carried out. His charismatic personality attracted the innocent young females who eventually became his victims. He approached them in public places, feigning injury or disability, or impersonating an authority figure. Finally the serial killer was executed by electric chair at age 42 *to the relief of American women.*

It is hard to imagine this same guy once volunteered at the Seattle office of Nelson Rockefeller's presidential campaign, attended the Republican National Convention in Miami as a Rockefeller delegate, took a job at Seattle's Suicide Hotline crisis center, became an honor student, well-regarded by his professors at UW, joined Governor Daniel J. Evans's reelection campaign and hired as an assistant to Ross Davis, Chairman of the Washington State Republic Party!

John Wayne Gacy Jr.

His criminal life was dominated by sexual assaults and murders of many teenage boys and young men, however, the smoke screens and his pathological lying became a major part of the perpetuation of these vicious crimes. These murders were committed inside his Norwood Park ranch house, victims were typically lured to his address by force or deception. Convicted, he was finally executed by lethal injection.

Again, it is hard to believe Gacy, at age of 18 became involved in politics, worked as an assistant precinct captain for a Democratic

Party candidate in his neighborhood, joined the Jaycees and named Key Man for the organization, risen to the position of vice-president of the Springfield Jaycees and named as the third most outstanding Jaycee within the State of Illinois, considered gregarious and helpful by the neighbors, appointed to serve upon the Norwood Park Township street lighting committee, subsequently earned the title of precinct captain, earned membership in a local Moose Club, became known as the "Killer Clown" because of his charitable services at fundraising events where he would dress as "Pogo the Clown", a character he devised himself, appointed director of Chicago's annual Polish Constitution Day Parade and photographed with a First Lady. She signed the photo, "To John Gacy. Best wishes. Rosalynn Carter."

Scott Peterson

He was described "very kind, very genteel," "dependable, well-disciplined," "more mature than most, pleasant to deal with." Only after he was found guilty of murdering his pregnant wife, opinions changed—"Liar," "A master manipulator who lacked the capacity to feel remorse or consider consequences"—"What lurked beneath charming veneer—a psychopathic (sociopathic) personality."

On Christmas Eve 2002, Scott reported his wife Laci missing. Suspicions grew when inconsistencies emerged in his story as well as his outright lies—Extramarital affairs, most recently with a massage therapist named Amber Frey—He told Frey *14 days before wife disappeared* that he'd "lost his wife" and that he would be spending his first Christmas without her—In the days after Laci went missing, he lied to Frey that he had traveled to Paris to celebrate the holidays—In reality, he had made one of these phone calls while attending the New Year's Eve candlelight vigil in Modesto for Laci. At the time of his arrest, Scott's hair and goatee had been bleached blonde. He claimed the lighter hair color was the result of chlorine from swimming in a friend's pool, however, according to the friend he had never swum in it.

Penny Boudreau

She is a different bird, seemingly nothing in common Bundy or Gacy, however turned to a callous liar after the killing of her own daughter to save the relationship with her boyfriend. After reporting to the police her 12-year-old daughter Karissa was missing, later at a press conference, she made a tearful plea to Karissa to come home. At a second emotional appeal to her daughter, she asked anybody who knew where she was to make contact. "It's hard not to know where your kid is," she told the reporters. Eyes swollen from crying, face pale and drawn, she said, "I'm trying not to think the worst. It's plain and simple hell. Not knowing where your kids are is horrible." The show went on for a while. She had driven her daughter to a deserted wooded area, knocked her to the ground and strangled her, ignored her terrified daughter's cries of 'Mummy, don't!'

Mini-Versions

Our ability to identify the mega-monsters in a timely manner is not good at all. Hopefully, the horrible ones like Bundy or Gacy will never be born again! However, different versions of Petersons and Boudreaus are likely to show up from time to time, the lying part emerging either before or after the crime. Every community is likely to have their smaller versions, growing up quietly, stealing from grandma's purse without remorse or grabbing Xanax from grandpa's medicine cabinet, and if caught have the instinctive tendency to lie about it with a straight face. These behaviors are likely to spread it wings, may be as shoplifting at the corner store or coning a classmate for money with promise to return it.

Even as adults, it may not be easy to identify them as crooks. It can very well be a charismatic college graduate or smart-looking computer technician or successful salesman with charming manners, or a recent arrival in town driving around in an expensive car, looking to take advantage of innocent people. They may fall short of the minimum three criteria needed to diagnose the Antisocial Personality Disorders and end up having only a *Mind Problem*, however, capable of causing devastations and disruptions to their lives and of those associated with them.

Warning Signs

In spite of the difficulties in identifying these monsters of different grades, those who look carefully may find certain warning signs. In the *Huffington Post Science* 2013 article written by Macrine Cooper-White, "11 Signs You May Be Dating a Sociopath", the writer asks, "Can that amazing new person you or a loved one is dating actually be a sociopath? It's not as far-fetched as you may imagine." Just with Antisocial Personality Disorder, the prevalence rates have been estimated between 0.2% and 3.3%. According to Harvard psychologist Dr. Martha Stout, author of *The Sociopath Next Door*, roughly one in 25 Americans is a sociopath.

The Post article went on to say, "Of course, not all sociopaths are dangerous criminals. But they certainly can make life difficult, given that the defining characteristic of sociopathy is antisocial behavior." It listed the Red Flags to look out for:

- Having an oversized ego. They tend to blame others for their own failures
- Lying and exhibiting manipulative behavior
- Exhibiting a lack of empathy. Absence of meaningful emotions
- Showing a lack of remorse or shame
- Staying eerily calm in scary or dangerous situations
- Behaving irresponsibly or with extreme impulsivity
- Having few friends
- Being charming—but only superficially
- Living by the "pleasure principle"
- Showing disregard for societal norms
- Having "intense" eyes

Waiting for the all the red flags to emerge may be too late. Intense eyes? No way! The guy had most of the signs, but not that kind of eyes. They may stay eerily calm in scary or dangerous situation? No. Our guy is not like that at all. He panics worse than a 10-year-old! The con-artists exhibit a pattern of concerning behaviors, however, in some situations one significant incident may be all that needed to prompt action by the victim.

Lying

A common thread connecting the sociopaths, and those with conduct disorders, antisocial personality disorders and even the *Antisocial Mind Problem* is lying. They thrive on it, believing they will never be caught! However, if it happened, there would be no hesitation to fabricate another one, not really caring others believed or not. It can be as simple as buying a porno magazine without spouse knowing about it or as serious as professing unconditional love to wife while carrying on an affair with an old girlfriend. When confronted, he is likely to become infuriated or even may try to play smart one more time!

It is not easy to catch a smart liar. What many people believe, can be simply wrong with the suspected clues—the facial change—lack of eye contact—being fidgety—rubbing the nose—hesitancy in answering and so on. According to Leanne ten Brinke, psychologist at the University of California at Berkeley whose work focused on detecting deception, these were old wives' tales. "The empirical literature just doesn't bear that out." Psychologist Paul Ekman at U.C. San Francisco spent many years studying nonverbal expressions of emotion and deception. In his research, he had more than fifteen thousand subjects watch video clips of people either lying or telling the truth. He found that their success rate at identifying honesty was approximately fifty-five percent. The nature of the lie or truth didn't even matter. The bottom line, our ability to tell a lie from the truth is hardly different from chance.

Fact Checking

Anytime there are inconsistencies and contradictions in the given story, it is time to take action, more so if there is a pattern of this degrading behavior. It may happen while dating someone on whom you have no background knowledge or hiring someone without good references. Revealing themselves honestly, for these people would be like standing in middle of the street naked. While trying to establish the conjugal relationship, their thoughts would be—Why do you want to know about my parents?—Siblings! None of your business—My previous jobs! What matters is what I have now—Don't ask me too many questions.

Fact checking can be complicated, however it is the best way to expose the liar. It should include not only the family connections and previous jobs, but also the educational record and places lived before. Previous relationships and legal problems may be covered up or deflated. They likely to consider if any past DWIs or shop lifting or any other atrocious behaviors in public records as untouchable subjects, with the sole intention to keep today's illusionary tranquility as intact as possible.

Taming them

How should someone antisocial be managed? The American generation that followed the real Ted Bundy story had a ready answer—fry him in the electric chair! Unfortunately, severe antisociality is hard to crack open and pour in good judgement. A St. Louis man forced to give up his antisocial adventures only after he became blind in a police shooting! The families often become the primary target of these monsters, exhausting the family members emotionally and financially too. It should not surprising that sometimes the relief came only when the beloved son or daughter got locked up in prison!

With such serious prognosis, it is important for the families to identify the future antisocials, even the mini-ones, when they are young and bring them to the attention of mental health experts. If they did not play their expected roles, the responsibility would fall upon the schools that also have to put up with these troublesome young population. It is not uncommon for the Family Services and even the legal system to get involved due to ongoing family pathology. In this day and age, many of these teenagers may have become victims of substance abuse that emerges as an innocent adventure, more of a *Mind Problem*. The management would consist of individual and family counseling, behavior modification strategies and substance abuse treatment as appropriate.

Medications

The child psychiatrists as well as adult psychiatrists often prescribe psychotropic medications for this patient population, sometimes simply begged by distraught families, who are exhausted taking care of these thugs. Since there are no FDA approved drugs for antisocial behavior, such treatment will target certain symptoms of this behavior and on any comorbidity.

Often the main concerns are likely to be impulsivity and aggressiveness. Mood stabilizers as lithium, anticonvulsants as carbamazepine and antipsychotics as risperidone are widely used for this purpose. Alpha-2 agonists, clonidine and guanfacine, as well as propranolol, buspirone and trazodone have been found effective in this patient populations. Those with ADHD, OCD and depressive and anxiety disorders may benefit from the appropriate treatments.

PART III
BRAIN OR MIND PROBLEM

CHAPTER 19
PILL POPPERS

In 2001, one of the most recognized talk show hosts in the nation signed a nine-year contract with Premiere Radio Networks, which syndicated his show to nearly 600 stations, for a total salary package reported to exceed $200 million. It was estimated, he had nearly 20 million listeners daily. He told his listeners, "Drug use, some might say, is destroying this country... And so, if people are violating the law by doing drugs, they ought to be accused and they ought to be convicted and they ought to be sent up." He also stated, "Too many whites are getting away with drug use" and drug trafficking, and proposed that the racial disparity in drug enforcement could be fixed if authorities increased detection efforts, conviction rates, and jail time for whites involved in illegal drugs.

About two years later, it became public knowledge that this talk-show host, Rush Limbaugh, was being investigated for illegally obtaining prescription drugs oxycodone and hydrocodone. Limbaugh told his audience "I need to tell you today that part of what you have heard and read is correct. I am addicted to prescription pain medication. I am not making any excuses. —I am no role model. I refuse to let anyone think I am doing something great here, when there are people you never hear about, who face long odds and never resort to such escapes. They are the role models." He also stated his addiction to painkillers resulted from several years of severe back pain heightened by a botched surgery intended to correct this problem.

Pill Abuse

The National Institute on Drug Abuse defines addiction as a chronic, relapsing brain disease characterized by the compulsive drug seeking and use, despite harmful consequences. The public knowledge about addictions at this time is high, bombarded by the media round the clock. However, most of it is confined to the alcohol and illicit drugs, the addiction to prescription drugs getting the due attention only recently.

Richard Kerlikowske, a national expert on addiction, pointed out, "The abuse of prescription drugs is our nation's fastest-growing drug problem." Nora Volkow, an expert in alcohol and drug abuse said, "Humans, in my view, will always want to experiment with things to make them feel good." Did it mean, addiction, well planted in human genes would be a part of us forever?

Prescription drug abuse is widespread and often begins as a common *Mind Problem*, innocently started to feel good, to do better, for genuine discomfort or, simply out of curiosity. However, in those with an addictive personality, the dangerous winds would be waiting to flare up the fire. Tolerance kicks in with the repeated usage, leaving the person needing more and more to receive the same reward. Nobody is immune from it, not even the King!

Elvis

The King of Rock 'n' Roll was born in a tiny, two-room shotgun house, built by his grandfather in anticipation of the little man's arrival. He grew up within a warm and close-knit family, all of them living near to one another. He was close to his parents, more so with his mother, and attended an Assembly of God church regularly. It was in the church that he found his musical inspiration and took basic guitar lessons from the church pastor.

In 1956, the Memphis man exploded on to the national music stage through the RCA single *Heartbreak Hotel* and rest was history. As years passed by, in the glare of public admiration, his priorities in life changed. The money pouring in, wealth building up, moving into a mansion, fan base expanding and his name becoming well-known all over the world, took a toll on him. His marriage failed and he developed an addiction to prescription medications. His primary physician, George C. Nichopoulos, explained Elvis's pill philosophy, he "felt that by getting (drugs) from a doctor, he wasn't the common everyday junkie getting something off the street."

Journalist Tony Scherman wrote, "Elvis Presley had become a grotesque caricature of his sleek, energetic former self. Hugely overweight, his mind dulled by the pharmacopoeia he daily ingested, he was barely able to pull himself through his abbreviated concerts." The half-hearted measures he took to redeem himself to his old, noble ways simply did not work. The decline was rapid and the end tragic. If he had kicked his prescription habit and regained his lost composure, who knows, he might be alive today, only 82 years old!

On the evening of August 16, 1977, Elvis was scheduled to fly out of Memphis; however, that afternoon he was found unresponsive on the bathroom floor of Graceland mansion. The attempts to revive him failed. He was only 42 years old. The lab reports suggested too many pills was the cause of his death. He had fourteen drugs in his system, ten in significant quantity!

Fallen Celebrities

Being a celebrity is a double-edged sword, enjoying the fame, glamor and wealth with it, at the same time being under the public scrutiny more than desired. If the evolution of celebrity began on shaky grounds, it would become even harder to stay above the fray and remain level-headed. To achieve certain equilibrium in their lives, some begin using prescription pills to provide the calmness and comfort, with the vicious monster addiction waiting in the wings. Celebrity pills are exactly the same kind of pills ordinary folks consume, and they too same fallacy, these pills can't be all that bad since they come from physicians.

Marilyn Monroe, Hollywood actress, model, and singer who became a major sex symbol, succumbed to these powerful pills and met an early death at age 36. With a mentally ill mother and after spending much of her childhood in foster homes, she began a career as a model, which led to a film contract in 1946 with Twentieth Century-Fox and the rest is public knowledge. Monroe had three unhappy marriages, the first one soon after she turned 16 to a sheet-metal worker, the second to New York Yankee legend Joe DiMaggio and the third to playwright and screenwriter Arthur Miller. The final years of Monroe's life were marked by illness, personal problems and pill abuse. The lady who lamented "Try to enjoy myself when I can—I'll be miserable enough as it is" was found dead at her home in Brentwood, Los Angeles on August 5, 1962. Toxicology studies revealed pentobarbital and chloral hydrate in her body.

Australian television and film actor Heath Andrew Ledger came to the U.S. in 1998 to develop a film career and worked in nineteen films. In 2005, he won the New York Critics Circle Award for Best Actor and, the following year, received Best International Actor Award from the Australian Film Institute. In a New York Times interview, he spoke of his recently completed roles in two films and the toll it took on his sleep, "Last week I probably slept an average of two hours a night-- I couldn't stop thinking. My body was exhausted, and my mind was still going." He admitted taking sleeping pills, sometimes more than prescribed.

In the afternoon of January 22, 2008, Ledger was found unconscious in his bed, attempts to revive him failed and the 28-year-old was pronounced dead. The Medical Examiner released a report that said, "Mr. Heath Ledger died as the result of acute intoxication by the combined effects of oxycodone, hydrocodone, diazepam, alprazolam, and doxylamine. We have concluded that the manner of death is accident, resulting from the abuse of prescription medications."

Anna Nicole Smith gained popularity by becoming Playmate of the Year and her marriage to business tycoon J. Howard Marshall, 63 years her senior. After his death, she engaged in a lengthy legal battle over his estate, modeled for clothing companies, starred in her own reality TV show, *The Anna Nicole Show,* and faced media scrutiny over the death of her son. Her own life ended tragically from an overdose of prescription drugs at age 39. Her death was ruled accidental, caused from *combined drug intoxication,* with the sleeping pill chloral hydrate as the major component. She had several other drugs in her system including diazepam, clonazepam, lorazepam, oxazepam, topiramate and Benadryl, all legitimate prescription medications.

Michael Jackson was born as the eighth child of a talented family and debuted on the professional music scene, along with his brothers, at age 6. However, later he turned solo and became a dominant figure in popular music. His music videos became household names and helped the television channel MTV to pick up popularity. His 1982 album *Thriller* became the bestselling album of all time.

Through the fame and fortune, a personal side of Michael Jackson began to emerge that included his changing appearance and family feuds. He was in total shock when accused of child sexual abuse and preferred to settle the case out of court for an undisclosed amount. In 2005, another accusation emerged and he was tried this time, however acquitted. The humiliation suffered in public was huge and took an emotional toll on this talented man. He took comfort in prescription medications and even had a personal physician to help him out. It was the medications, Propofol and a benzodiazepine, provided by the doctor that led to the death of the King of Pop at the age of 50.

Prince, the singer-songwriter, actor, multi-instrumentalist, dancer and record producer became another celebrity victim of medication overdose on April 21, 2016. A press release from the Midwest Medical Examiner's Office in Anoka County stated that the 57-year-old, one of the best-selling artists of all time had died of an accidental overdose of fentanyl.

What happened to these famous people were the glaring, sad examples of prescription medication abuse that began innocently as everyday mind problems, not as disorder or disease. Physicians, often mesmerized by the fame and money of their customers, played a part in these tragedies. However, there are numerous celebrities who successfully managed their addictions and even tried to help others in need.

Survivors

Elizabeth Taylor, the Hollywood Queen, acknowledged her own addiction to prescription drugs, and was concerned about her friend Michael Jackson's medication problems. During the dedication of the Elizabeth Taylor Medical Center, she said, "I have suffered and dealt with the same kind of medical problems now affecting my friend Michael Jackson. Because of my own experience with addiction to prescription medicines, I was able to make a number of calls in search of the best and the most appropriate treatment for him." Interestingly, Jackson himself had expressed his fears that he would end up just like Elvis!

Betty Ford, First Lady of the United States during the presidency of her husband Gerald Ford, was another celebrity who faced twin demons of opioid pain pills and alcohol, recovered from them and became the founder of the Betty Ford Center for substance abuse and addiction. She revealed that her addiction to pain pills began with getting the prescriptions for a pinched nerve. She wrote in her memoir, "I liked alcohol. It made me feel warm. And I loved pills. They took away my tension and my pain."

Actress and author Jamie Lee Curtis opened up about her own addiction to pain meds. "I, too, found painkillers after a routine cosmetic surgical procedure and I, too, became addicted, the morphine becomes the warm bath from which to escape painful reality. I was a lucky one. I was able to see that the pain had started long ago and far away and that finding the narcotic was merely a matter of time. The pain needed numbing. My recovery from drug addiction is the single greatest accomplishment of my life... but it takes work—hard, painful work—but the help is there, in every town and career—" Her 1998 book, *Today I Feel Silly, and Other Moods That Make My Day*, made the best-seller list in The New York Times.

Nation of Pill Poppers

America has the unsavory title *Nation of Pill Poppers* due to a unique love affair with their medications, mostly good; however, leading to health problems as well on a massive scale. According to the *Health, United States 2013* data, the number of Americans who had taken at least one prescription drug in the month prior to the survey was close to half the population. A study published in the journal Mayo Clinic Proceedings reported even much higher numbers. Their researchers found nearly 70 percent of Americans were on at least one prescription drug, more than half of them taking two, and one in five were on five or more of meds!

Such data raises several legitimate questions: With 50 to 70 percent of the U.S. population consuming prescription medications, do Americans live longer? According to WHO 2013 world ranking on life expectancy, the U.S. was ranked 34th. Were Americans in more pain than the rest of the world? The CDC reported the U.S. that had only 4.6 percent of the world's population consumed 80 percent of the world supply of opioids. Even worse than the above numbers is each year millions of people use medications prescribed for someone else. This unfortunate social trend causes injuries and deaths, too. The most abused prescription drugs across the population fall under three categories—opioids, tranquilizers and stimulants. They are obtained:

- Free from a friend or relative; 54 percent
- Being purchased or taken; 17 percent
- From a physician; 18 percent
- Coming from more than one physician; 2 percent
- From a drug dealer or stranger; 4 percent
- On the internet; 0.3 percent

The rest was not clearly identified. Unlike other addictions, the prescription drug addiction is very unique, since physicians are often involved but may not be fully aware of what is unfolding. In spite of the best intentions, many meds end up in the wrong hands. The National Institute on Drug Abuse (NIDA) estimates 20 percent of the U.S population 12 years and older have used prescription drugs for nonmedical reasons at least once in their lifetimes, young people strongly represented in this group.

In a survey of high school students asking if they ever took prescription drugs without a doctor's permission, one in five said yes! They preferred prescription drugs more than street drugs, believing in their safety. One added danger of the prescription drug abuse, according to the National Center on Addiction and Substance Abuse, is that teens who abuse them are twice as likely to use alcohol, five times more likely to use marijuana, and twelve to twenty times more likely to use illegal street drugs.

Joy Plant

The most powerful, addictive medications are opiates, found naturally in the opium poppy plant, what Sumerians referred to it as *Hul Gil*, the joy plant. Its cultivation dates back to at least the Neolithic age and almost all human civilizations evolved since then used it lavishly for pleasure and rituals and relief from severe pains. Galen, the Great physician, wrote about poppy juice and recommended it for headaches, deafness, epilepsy, asthma, coughs, colic, fevers, women's problems and melancholy!

Confessions of an English Opium-Eater written by Thomas de Quincey revealed the early days of Turkish natives of Constantinople who regularly drank a black water made with opium that made them feel good, but to which they became so addicted, if they tried to go without, they would quickly die! Wars were waged over opium between China and the East India Company of Great Britain. U.S. physicians and pharmacists dispensed opium to women with female problems in abundance. During the American Civil War, the Union Army used opium tincture and powder and about 500,000 opium pills to treat the wounded in pain. Due to its popularity, the users called it *God's Own Medicine!*

In 1817, pure morphine was isolated from opium. This was followed by isolation of codeine, synthesis of heroin, introduction of oxycodone, emergence of methadone, pethidine and fentanyl. Opiates with a long track record continued to dominate pain management not only with older productions, but also through newer semi-synthetic and synthetic variations.

The CDC reported that U.S healthcare providers wrote 259 million prescriptions for opioid painkillers in 2012 alone. Almost all specialty physicians prescribed them, however, the numbers were the highest for primary care doctors, internists and dentists. Another startling number was 80 percent of all prescription pain killers were written by roughly 20 percent of the prescribers! Using the number of prescriptions written as a yardstick to measure the extent and severity of pain, the National Institute on Drug Abuse came up with this startling and interesting data:

- Men are more in pain than women!
- Caucasians are more in pain than other races or ethnicities!
- Those who lived in rural areas are more in pain than those in urban neighborhoods!
- Middle-aged people are more in pain that older folks!
- Those who lived in Southern United States are more in pain than rest of the country!

The highest number of opioid prescriptions were generated in Alabama, Tennessee, and West Virginia. The opioid prescriptions were 143 per 100 people in Alabama, while only 52 for every 100 people in Hawaii. They have become the new brand of *heroin* that can be obtained much more easily from several sources including physicians.

On average, 82 people die daily in the U.S. as the result of taking too much opioid pain medication. Not surprisingly, the states with poorer prescription-control laws and most painkiller sales per person had the most deaths. These overdoses kill more people than car accidents in 17 states, an ugly milestone reached in American history! The public health and law enforcement officials in the Obama administration present the data in different way, pointing out that painkillers are now responsible for more deaths than crack in the 1980s and black tar heroin in the 1970s combined.

Benzos

Benzodiazepines, the Benzos dominated the 1960's Western World, first came Librium, soon followed by Valium. Doctors happily prescribed these meds since they were a vast improvement upon the barbiturates and similar drugs used previously to treat anxiety. Patients felt comfortable in taking them without the usual stigma attached to psych medications. However, just as Valium was receiving publicity due to its usage by famous people and entering the medicine cabinets of even conservative, middle-class, suburban families, it, as well other benzodiazepines that followed like Xanax, Ativan and Klonopin, were establishing notoriety for ruining lives due to their addictive ability. A large-scale study in the U.S. conducted by the Substance Abuse and Mental Health Services Administration determined that benzodiazepines were present in more than 28 percent of emergency department visits involving the nonmedical use of pharmaceuticals, a significant number of which were suicide attempts. The data from the National Vital Statistics System multiple cause-of-death file from 2010 showed that benzodiazepines were involved in 29 percent of deaths, usually mixed with alcohol and other drugs.

Sleep Aids

Americans, well-known for their long working hours, who wanted
to wind down at the end of the day, often used alcohol to sedate themselves; however, some preferred sleeping pills to calm down their restless minds. Data from the National Health and Nutrition Examination
Survey, 2005– 2010, revealed that about 4 percent of U.S. adults aged
20 and older used them to go to sleep, this percentage increased with
the age and education. The higher usage was among women and Cau-
casian population. However, all was not rosy with their usage, many
taking too much, too long and some obtaining them without prescription. In 2011, there were 30,149 emergency room visits due to nonmedical use of the popular sleeping pill Ambien alone.
    Another surprising concern with sleeping pills is the higher mor-
tality rates associated with even their regular usage. Daniel Kripke at
the University of California, San Diego School of Medicine examined
five years of electronic medical records collected by a health system
in Pennsylvania, comparing more than 10,000 patients who had been
prescribed a sleep medicine, most commonly Ambien, and more than
20,000 patients who had not and published his findings in the *British Medical Journal*. After adjusting for varying factors Kripke found
that people who had taken sleeping pills were more than three times
as likely to have died during the study period as those who had not.
Those on higher doses of the drugs were more than five times as likely
to have died.

Stimulants

    Which group of drugs can enhance alertness and concentration,
counteract lethargy and fatigue, depress appetite and promote weight
loss, improve depressed mood and sadness, reduce hyperactivity and
treat narcolepsy? The answer is psychostimulants like Adderall. Even in
U.S. their usage largely influenced by local culture and socio-economic
factors. There was no surprise when Medco Health Solutions recently reported that the sales of prescription stimulants had quintupled
since 2002. And, the *New York Times* reported, the number of Ritalin

180   C.J. JOS

and Adderall prescriptions written for active-duty service members increased by nearly 1,000 percent in five years!

A 2009 study by the National Survey on Drug Use and Health pointed out the unfortunate trend of psychostimulants, especially Adderall which was widely abused on college campuses. It was also found that the individuals using Adderall non-medically were three times more likely to have used marijuana in the past year, eight times more likely to have used cocaine and anxiety pills, and five times more likely to have used painkillers improperly. Ninety percent of those who abused Adderall reported binge drinking and more than 50 percent were heavy drinkers.

Managing It

Addiction is an enormous, complex problem, part of it emerging from the brain and other part from the mind. Once this viper begins squeezing the rabbit, it is hard for the little animal to escape from its hold. Even intensive treatment in the most prestigious addiction treatment centers, attending well-conducted AA meetings, actively taking part in well-organized methadone and suboxone programs or getting the vivitrol injections monthly may not be enough for everyone to escape from its dark shadows. The only one hundred percent successful solution is prevention

Children should be taught the medicine hygiene from a young age, even with the usage of a pill for fever or headache. In houses with youngsters, the medicine cabinet should be kept locked and monitored periodically, to make sure no unauthorized person has access to it. Parents, even if they have their own demons facing them, are still obliged to teach their children of the good, bad and ugly aspects of medications.

William S. Burroughs, the American novelist and short story writer, asked, "Why does a man become a drug addict? The answer is that he usually does not intend to become an addict. You don't wake up one morning and decide to be a drug addict—Most addicts--did not start using drugs for any reason they can remember. They just drifted along until they got hooked."

For many teenagers, drug use starts in a fun, social setting as a form of recreation or social bonding. It can easily happen in school bathrooms or may be in gym. One young person befriending another with a pill that may have come from the medicine cabinet of grandparents or from the senior selling it for a small profit. The victim's pleasured brain cells will code the experience for future reference!

In its early stages, drug use for all practical purposes, will be more of an everyday mind problem than a disease, generating pleasure as well as guilt, missing school here and there, calling in sick at work once in a while and wondering if the angry outburst at home was caused by it. However, with full confidence, they will think "I can control its use." However, after continued usage, the addictive tentacles spread and the squeeze begins to be felt in all facets of life.

With higher concerns about opioids, there have been public attempts to contain this American tragedy. A recent FDA funded study showed that the number of hydrocodone prescriptions fell after the DEA reclassified them from Schedule III to the more restrictive Schedule II of the Controlled Substance Act. Most of the decline, 74 percent, was attributable to a significant reduction in refills.

A Private Policy

Still, it is important for each individual to have a *private policy* in dealing with the addictive medications. This policy should consist of:

- Never use a medicine without prescription
- Never use a medicine prescribed for someone else
- Check with the physician/pharmacist if concerned about a prescribed addictive medicine
- Always use caution with taking addictive drugs. The risk of developing addiction will be higher with bigger doses and long-term usage, and in those having or had an alcohol or drug problem. The risk is low in those who take as needed with permission of the physician for a short period of time
- Be honest with the prescriber, if an addictive medication required. Asking for such a medication may raise a red flag for some physicians, however, it would not necessarily mean a definite denial. Even for a person with addictive personality, depending on

circumstances, the doctor may consider usage for a shorter period of time, providing smaller quantities, encouraging the use only as needed rather than taking every day and, occasionally, even authorizing a family member to monitor the medication

• If in chronic pain, enquire into non-opiate options or even non-medication means for pain control. This should always come as the first line of treatment in chronic pain

• If in chronic anxiety, enquire about non-medication means to alleviate it or asking for non-addictive medications to control it

• Avoid taking two sedative drugs at the same time, like an opioid for pain control and a benzo like Xanax for anxiety

• Avoid taking a stimulant and a downer at the same time, like Adderall with Xanax

• Avoid using prescription sleeping pills on a long term basis

The initial decision to take an addictive medication may be voluntary, however, with continued use, a person's ability to exert self-control gets seriously impaired and such a loss is the hallmark of addiction. Brain imaging studies of people with addiction have shown changes in the areas of the brain critical to judgment, decision making, learning and memory. The addiction can begin as an everyday *Mind Problem*, but slowly turns into a disease, not caring if its victim was a cultural icon or a famous radio host or a suburban housewife or a hard-working family man.

CHAPTER 20
ONLY BEER

The consumption of alcohol has been a part of humanity forever, this solid liquid-link connecting the ancient cultures to our modern times. In primitive rituals, it was used by the holy men to please their Gods, medicine men to cleanse the wounds and comfort those in pain. The usage continued through millenniums, its benefits as well as harmful effects discussed and debated by the religious pundits, esteemed philosophers, social activists and well-spirited politicians.

Today, in most cultures, alcohol has become an integral part of family celebrations, community festivals and victory ovations. In the Western world, it is hard to imagine a wedding reception without at least a cash-bar, Christmas without lavish food and appropriate alcoholic beverage. As a social lubricant, people generally feel more relaxed after consuming this liquid and less self-conscious, and so, many social functions are built around its consumption.

Among the various forms of alcoholic drinks, beer gained a special place in many homes by becoming a part of everyday life, especially among men. It is not unusual to have a large fridge in the garage filled with cold ones, considered only as thirst quenchers, and some will go for one as soon they reach home from a hard day's work, preferring beer to the tasteless water or so-so coke. Some brave souls will even exhibit their machismo by sipping one in the morning, instead of coffee or tea!

At neighborhood parties and July 4th get-togethers, there is often loud discussions about the weather of the day, rain chances and politics, and also about their favorite beer. Some men even venturing into the details of taste and texture, pitching the qualities and benefits of one versus the other, ale and lager, Busch and Miller, English and German, hybrid and specialties, periodically picking up a cold one from the ice-filled coolers. However, there would hardly ever any dialogue about the buzz from the cold ones, since that was strictly a private matter!

Time for a Beer

On December 5, 1933, at 6:55 p.m., when President Franklin D. Roosevelt's signature ratified the Twenty-First Amendment bringing down Prohibition across the land, he said, "I believe this would be a good time for a beer." Beer drinking has been part of the American culture, whether barbequing in the backyard, attending a favorite baseball game, playing golf in the city park, or even enjoying at a church picnic. Singer Luke Bryan's "Drink a Beer" or Country Music Hall of Famer Hank Thompson's single "Six Pack to Go" did not shy away from this subject. Bernie Mac described his heaven on earth, "When I get a chance—to go on a boat with good people, take the boat out and put some lobsters on the grill, get the ice-cold beer and the cigars."

There are many people who believe that they would not become alcoholics if they only imbibed the cold ones. Brainwashed by this philosophy, the beer-people are more likely to describe themselves as social drinkers, and for them it is not a big deal if they have one or two in the evening, or even if their kid has a sip of this liquid on special occasions. Some even brag about it, believing a drink at home with supervision would not allow their son or daughter to turn to alcoholism. However, for many kids who later became alcoholics, their first taste of alcohol was beer! With this concern, CDC answered the question, is beer safer to drink than liquor? NO-NO-NO. One 12-ounce beer has about the same amount of alcohol as 1.5-ounce shot of liquor. It is the amount of alcohol consumed that affects a person most, not the type of alcoholic drink.

Drinkers

Alcohol users come from all backgrounds, gender, education, and socio-economic status not providing any protection from its ill effects. What they drinking may be beer or wine, hard liquor of their choice or a specially prepared cocktail. Irrespective of it, all of them can be placed in a defined category either by their own free will or brought on by the events that happened beyond their control. Generally, these are based on the severity of drinking, functionality of the drinker, and the social and health consequences brought on by it.

The *social drinker* is defined as 'the person who drinks in moderation, drinks occasionally, never gets into any kind of trouble because of it, doesn't do or say things while drinking that are regretted later, feels no need to control alcohol intake and never worries about having to cut back.' This form of drinking is considered a private affair even in a public setting, never leaving any black marks for others to see.

National Institute on Alcohol Abuse and Alcoholism (NIAAA) identifies another group of those with *low-risk drinking*, for females this consists of no more than 7 drinks per week and no more than 3 drinks per sitting. For males, it consists of no more than 14 drinks per week and no more than 4 drinks per day.

For most people, the progression of drinking occurs over a long time period, many downplay this trend. However, others can identify them due to their outlandish behaviors under the influence, relationship problems and entanglements with the law, inability to pursue education and hold down jobs. Some get the shock of their life with a diagnosis of liver or pancreatic ailment from their doctor, or enforced with DWI or jail term for public disturbance under the influence from legal authorities. NIAAA identified one group of *problem drinkers*, those who have a single period of heavy drinking that lasts 3-4 years and peaks at ages 18-24, typically occurs during the college years, and then they phase out of it. When problem drinkers are given sufficient reason to cut back on their drinking, they are able to return to drinking in a low-risk manner.

Alcoholics are identified as those unable to permanently cut back on their drinking. They may have had occasions where they drank in a low-risk manner, but they inevitably return to their alcoholic drinking patterns. What does end-stage alcoholism look like? In *end-stage alcoholism*, such person is consumed by drinking, withdrawal symptoms and years of daily drinking make it incredibly difficult to stop. By this time the disease has grossly affected the health and functionality of such people.

George E. Vaillant described two multi-decade studies of the lives of 600 American males, non-alcoholics at the outset, focusing on their lifelong drinking behaviors. By following the men from youth to old age, it was possible for him to chart their drinking patterns and what factors may have contributed to alcoholism. He observed that there was no sharp dividing line between alcoholics and non-alcoholics. The number of drinking problems was spread out along a scale, just like IQ and blood pressure; there was not a cluster of alcoholics at the top end of the scale. The author pointed out alcoholism had a gradual onset over 5 to 15 years of continuous alcohol abuse.

Early Sippers

A time-honored dictum in medicine that early onset chronic diseases are associated with worse prognosis holds well for alcoholism as well. There is the compelling scientific evidence that the early usage of alcohol can lead to alcohol abuse and dependence later in life. DeWit DJ and colleagues identified that critical age as 11 to 14 and published their data in the American Journal of Psychiatry. A study published in *Alcoholism: Clinical & Experimental Research* found that not only getting drunk, but also simple drinking at an early age was a key risk factor for continued alcohol abuse by high school students.

Roughly 30 percent of the students said that they had *tasted* alcohol when in sixth grade. Of that group of the *early sippers,* 26 percent reported having consumed a full alcoholic drink and 9 percent had gotten totally trashed by the ninth grade. According to the psychiatric diagnostic manual, the future alcoholic is likely to get drunk for the first time during mid-teen years, alcohol abuse peaking in late teens to early- mid-20s, with the vast majority of them developing alcoholism by their late 30s.

Scientists at the University of Vermont in Canada recently found that one glass of wine or a beer at the age of 14 could set teenagers on the path to binge drinking. The study predicted which 14 year olds taking part would end up binge drinkers by the age of 16, with 70 percent accuracy. Hugh Garavan, who co-led the study, said the vulnerable period between the ages of 14 and 16 was *critical* to a young person's future drinking behavior. "Just delaying people drinking by six months or a year is actually a very, very substantial intervention that would have vast beneficial consequences," he added.

In a long-term study by Brown University of 561 students in Rhode Island, researchers found the same trend with early exposure to alcohol. Lead researcher Kristina Jackson pointed out, "Parents who think that exposing their children to alcohol early on and in safe environments will somehow make them less likely to down an entire bottle of peach schnapps and jump naked into their friends' swimming pool, turns out, it's actually the other way around. Give the kiddies a taste of liquor, and it'll wet their chops—or at least falsely build their personal sense of worldliness."

All these should be a warning for the parents and grandparents who genuinely hope that by providing the drink at home, the young ones less likely to drink outside! Some take pride in providing *Johnny* or *Kathy* with an occasional beer, hoping to develop a special bond with the youngster—this is your birthday—you can have a cold one—make sure you do not do its own your own—today is July 4th—it won't hurt you to have a sip with your B-B-Q. Permitting to try alcohol at a young age send the wrong message that drinking is not that dangerous! Jackson stressed that in addition to the *early sipper* factor, the parents' drinking habits, a family history of alcoholism, and general personality and behavioral characteristics also have strong impact on the boozy worldviews of children and teenagers.

Media Hullabaloo

Even today there are those in the media proclaiming the benefits of beer drinking! Fox News Media published an article in 2014 under the title, "The Surprising Health Benefits of Beer," stating, "If you've got party plans this weekend, don't be afraid to knock back a cold one. Beer has several surprising health benefits. It actually has a number of natural antioxidants and vitamins that can help prevent heart disease and even rebuild muscle. It also has one of the highest energy contents of any food or drink. Of course, this means you need to set limits: one beer gets you going, four makes you fat."

In a 2015 article, Kristen Domonell wrote of the reasons to have a beer right now, "Sure, you probably have beer to thank for helping you meet your girlfriend, spurring some of your greatest stories, and bringing out your worst dance moves. But it turns out there are tons of other awesome, scientifically proven reasons to love a good brew. Beer could safeguard your heart, boost your immunity, protect your bones, and more. Ready, set, drink up."

Candace Nelson, a writer and editor wrote for *Health Lifestyle*,

"Unexpected Benefits of Beer That Give You Good Reasons To Drink It"—"A cold lager is refreshing on a summer afternoon. A crowd pleaser for all tastes and all seasons, also brings unexpected benefits—rich in B vitamins and high in fiber. A beer a day keeps stress and heart attacks away, lowers the risk of type 2 diabetes, lowers the risk of developing gallstones, has antimicrobial properties which could fight disease, is good for muscles, reduces the risk for Alzheimer's and is good for bone density."

Why People Drink?

Thirsty—I like the taste of it—It makes me relax. It is a social lubricant. Betty Ford wrote in her autobiography, "I liked alcohol. It made me feel warm." In spite of its wide availability, however, there are many people who will not drink it because—*don't like it—horrible taste, cannot stand it.* Is it a myth that the availability of alcohol alone enough to cause addiction?

Although everyone has the potential for addiction, some people are more predisposed to it than others. The high schoolers can easily identify some among them who drink *alcoholically* from the very beginning, out of control with no inhibitions, often seeming like a show off! Others start out as moderate drinkers and then become alcoholics later on. What was the difference between the two groups?

According to Francesca Ducci and colleagues from the National Institute on Alcohol Abuse and Alcoholism, the genetic factors account for 40 to 60 percent of the risk of alcoholism. The Scandinavian studies put this strong relationship on firm grounds, their twin study showing the risk was 60 percent for identical versus 39 percent for fraternal twins. In their adoption studies, when adopted in infancy and studied into adulthood, sons of alcoholics were four times as likely to be alcoholic as were the sons of non-alcoholics. And, this risk was not affected by the alcoholism status of the adopted parents.

Another way to look at this genetic risk, if one parent is alcoholic, the child has a 25 percent chance of having the disease, and if both parents alcoholics the risk doubles to 50 percent. The risk is three to four times higher in close relatives of alcoholics. Theodore Reich at Washington University in St. Louis studied alcoholic families and found 38 percent of the alcoholics had alcoholic fathers, 21 percent alcoholic mothers, 57 percent alcoholic brothers, 15 percent alcoholic sisters, 32 percent alcoholic sons and 19 percent alcoholic daughters.

The various genetic pathways affecting alcohol drinking have been investigated by Boris Tabakoff and his team at the University of Colorado-Denver. The researchers discovered that drinking behavior was linked to the *pleasure and reward* pathways in the brain and different genetic factors predisposed to alcohol dependence versus alcohol consumption, and emphasized on the interaction between genes and environment.

The power of genetics is so powerful, it has fooled many children of alcoholics who grew up believing that they never would become like their parent! However, they did exactly the same thing as they grew up, showing how strong the biology of brain was compared to the psychology of mind.

Many may be self-treating their underlying emotional problems, including the everyday mind problems, using alcohol. It relieves the stress at least temporarily, promotes sleep, increases appetite, makes it easier to meet strangers at the wedding reception and even improves the dancing rhythm to the joy of onlookers. Even though classified as a depressant, mental health professionals occasionally come across alcoholics who swear that they would become depressed and suicidal if they quit drinking!

Celebrity Drinkers

Just like anyone driving a vehicle is at the risk of having an accident, anyone consuming alcohol is at the risk of alcoholism. It begins as an enjoyable or adventurous behavior, becomes an everyday mind problem, before landing in the terrain of a clinical disorder. With no discrimination whatsoever, this viper bites people of every walk of life, not caring if the victim lived inside the luxury of White House or became a glittering star on television and movies or an influential member of congressional chambers at Washington or has won a Nobel Prize for the strong influence on 20th century fiction or landed back on earth from the moon! Their stories of struggles with addiction are the same as everyone else, none of them began drinking thinking about alcoholism. For most, it came on slowly, unheralded, as a social habit, part of a culture. Some succeed and became inspirational to many. Some failed unable to escape from the viper's hold.

Betty Ford, the wife of the 38th President of United States, Gerald Ford, opened up her private life of addiction to the public and earned much respect for doing so. For her, it began by taking pain pills for a pinched nerve; however, it gradually included alcohol as well. It would be exacerbated by what she viewed at the time as normal alcohol consumption, a routine among the cocktail parties which congressional couples were then expected to frequent.

In 1978 Betty Ford was confronted by the family on her problematic drinking and son Steven later described the scene, "He (father) took her hand and said, 'Betty, we love you. The kids want their mother back and I want my wife back.' We all cried and fought and got angry and hugged." Recognizing the alcoholism of her father, one of her brothers and her first husband, Betty Ford finally admitted that she had been in denial about her dependency on alcohol. Most with an alcohol problem will use denial as a means to rationalize their increasingly risky behavior.

Steven himself a victim of alcohol, described how he informed his mother of his own problem, "I went to her and I said, 'Mom, I think I am an alcoholic.' And she was just like every mother in the country. "Oh, no. My son, you can't be an alcoholic. She wanted to be in denial." Steven Ford achieved sobriety and became the chairman of the Gerald R. Ford Presidential Foundation. He paid high compliments to his mother when speaking at an anniversary gala for Gateway Rehabilitation Center in Pittsburgh. "A mother, who is a former first lady, and 30 years ago, she raised her hand and said, 'My name is Betty and I am an alcoholic,' which changed the face of alcoholism back in the late 70s."

Robin Williams rose to fame with his role in *Mork & Mindy*, subsequently becoming a stand-up comedian and performing in many feature films. The fame and fortune took a toll on him, and he struggled with alcoholism and cocaine abuse in the early 1980s but quit cold turkey after friend and fellow comedian John Belushi's fatal overdose. However, after two decades of sobriety and success in his career and family life, Williams fell off the wagon. "It's (addiction) not caused by anything, it's just there," he said. "It waits. It lays in wait for the time when you think, it's fine now, I'm OK. Then, the next thing you know, it's not OK. Then you realize, where am I? I didn't realize I was in Cleveland." Williams said that falling back into alcohol abuse was very gradual.

"It's the same voice thought that... you're standing at a precipice and you look down, there's a voice and it's a little quiet voice that goes, 'Jump,'" Williams told Diane Sawyer in 2006. "The same voice that goes, 'Just one.'... And the idea of just one for someone who has no tolerance for it, that's not a possibility." Williams said he had spent a couple of years thinking he could handle his alcohol problem on his own. "But you can't. That's the bottom line. You really think you can, then you realize, I need help, and that's the word. It's hard admitting it, then once you've done that, it's real easy. You think people don't notice. Then you find out later 'We knew.'... You went outside naked. No, I didn't. But even the dog was like 'What's wrong, boy?' Humiliation gives you humility." On August 11, 2014, Williams died at his home in Paradise Cay, California at the age of 63. The autopsy report confirmed the mode of death as suicide.

Joseph McCarthy, the man after whom the term *McCarthyism* was coined, made it his political mission to identify and eradicate the supposed subversive communists living in the United States during the Cold War. As a U.S. Senator he made wild accusations claiming the State Department and other parts of the U.S. federal government were infested with Soviet spies and sympathizers, made believable in an atmosphere of heightened paranoia of that era.

As he was ruining many innocent lives, he was also eroding his own with alcohol. In a book written after his death, journalist Richard Rovere described McCarthy as follows, "He had always been a heavy drinker, and there were times in those seasons of discontent when he drank more than ever. The difficulty toward the end was that he couldn't hold the stuff. He went to pieces on his second or third drink. And he did not snap back quickly." McCarthy was censured by the Senate in 1954. The shame of it made his drinking worse. A dark chapter in American history came to end with his death in 1957.

Ernest Hemingway, the American novelist, short story writer, and journalist, influenced 20th century fiction through his economical and understated style of writing and thrilled his generation through his public image of adventures on the war front and travels through continents. Many of his works are considered classics of American literature. The tormented writer considered alcohol a constant companion, with the work ethos, "Write drunk; edit sober." According to his biographer Kenneth Lynn, he would regularly drink "two or three bottles of liquor a day, as well as wine with meals" with less time to edit. Maybe the brilliant man did not need much time to edit! Suffering from depression as well, his life came to an end, tragically, in 1961. He was 62 years old.

Buzz Aldrin reached spectacular heights becoming the second man to walk on the moon; however, on earth he battled his own demons with alcohol. Later on, he told an audience that he had been an alcoholic leading up to the famed Apollo 11 flight in 1969. His drinking problem got worse, his life spiraled down with a break-up of his 21-year marriage and depression. Hitting rock bottom in 1978, he entered rehab to achieve total sobriety. He took up another mission in his life, helping those with alcohol problems.

Self-Made Problem?

Addiction, is it a self-made problem by the addicted person with full acknowledgement of the mind? Or, is it a brain disorder brought on by the neurons and neurotransmitters? Did the brain propose and the mind dispose? Today, scientists overwhelming support the view, addiction is a brain disorder in which the mind plays a very significant role. That is why, understanding both the brain and mind are important in managing the addictions. It is well-accepted that often it needs more than the will power to conquer this powerful monster. However, it becomes confusing to many since there is a willful part as well in it. The concept of *Self* did not want to hand over that control to some mysterious chemicals inside the brain, at least not the total control.

There would be many who try to copout without taking responsibility to the problem, instead blaming their brain illness making statements such as—

"I have a chemical imbalance."
"It's my brain chemistry. There is nothing I can do about it."
"It is in my genes. I can't help it."

Some people may even accuse the medical community of helping addicts get rid of their guilt by calling addiction a brain disorder! The brain scientists would be quick to point out, everyone using alcohol did not become alcoholics. Family and twin studies have shown that addiction affects those with genetic tendency to it. In fact, those with this predisposition, tended to feel less anxious, more euphoric, and energized with frequent use of chemical substances.

The brain chemistry changes with continued use of alcohol, some experts branding it as a neuro-toxin even in small amounts. If so, in large amounts the damage would be more profound. This brings up the question, can the abstinence from alcohol return the brain to its normal healthy state? Maybe in its early stages. For instance, quit smoking reduces the risk for lung cancer. The longer one goes without smoking, the lesser the risk of getting it. In the same way, the longer the abstinence from alcohol, the better would be the outcome. Once an addict, is the person addicted forever? The AA movement has a huge impact in the way addiction handled and treated. AA emphasizes that once an addict, such a person is an addict forever. There is convincing scientific evidence to support this viewpoint.

Risk Reduction

Many people consider social drinking a normal part of life, not something to be concerned about. However, this too has the potential to turn slowly to a significant mind problem, especially in those with genetic vulnerability, the disease of alcoholism waiting in the wings. Since prevention is a lot easier than curing the illness, anyone with a genetic risk should have a risk-reduction plan.

- Every family member at risk needs to know that the only sure way not to become an alcoholic is not consuming alcohol at all. Even youngsters should be educated of their genetic risk; the primary responsibility for doing so would be to the parents, grandparents and significant others. If they themselves face alcohol problem, even then, they have to be honest with the children and use their examples as way to educate the young ones. The school system also has the responsibility of educating the young population of the higher risk for complications in the early sippers
- Children should never be provided any form of alcohol includ-

ing beer, on the pretext that drinking at home would make them responsible drinkers later on. Any usage by them, even recreational, should be taken seriously. If they plan to drink at the appropriate age, educate them even more and introduce them to responsible drinking

• One way to keep the devil out of the fence is being happy in life, keeping busy through work, spending time with family, developing hobbies, indulging in recreational and physical activities, and practicing spirituality and religion, as appropriate. Alcoholics Anonymous teaches addicts the need for intervention by a higher power, without allowing them to go through the guilt trip

• Alcohol is a social lubricant and most people enjoy drinking in company. Those concerned about their drinking has to reevaluate their social relationships in this context, as part of risk reduction. Maybe the weekend drinking buddy should to be kept at a distance!

• Each person facing the risk has to have a well-thought-out plan—If alcoholic beverages should be kept at home? Should beer be stocked in the fridge, making it possible to gulp it at a moment's notice? Those who have a fashionable bar with colorful bottles adjacent to the family room or in the basement need to reevaluate its continued presence as a tempting factor

• Any negative comment about drinking that comes from others, spouse or friend, should be taken seriously. It's good time to think loud about the problem, instead of getting mad at the person who points it out

• Those who drink in excess should get a physical checkup at least once a year to catch any alcohol related illnesses early on, including liver and pancreas diseases, diabetes, hyperlipidemia and even certain forms of cancer.

Private Policy

If complete abstinence is not possible, every problem drinker struggling with this issue should at least have a private policy in place to make sure their drinking did not get out of control.

• Keep a health journal and honestly write down every *alcoholic incidence* for future reference, whether it is yelling at spouse, a hangover, missing work, an argument with neighbor and so on. The progression of these unpleasant events may give warning to the next stage of even more serious events—Accidents, DWI, loss of job, spouse threatening divorce and much more

• The beer drinker should keep a tab on how many cans or bottles they drink on an occasion and its progression through the years. One beer enjoyed with friends in high school, may have developed into a six-pack habit in college, getting worse slowly later in life

• Those who consume hard liquor should always pour it with a measuring cup and be consistent with it. The cup, plain or nicely decorated it did not matter, will never lie without your permission

• As a part of the private policy, each person has to recognize own triggering points to excessive drinking. It can be the anticipation of Friday evening after working hard for five long days, an upcoming vacation, July 4th, Christmas, high anxiety social situations and so on. Good strategies should be in place beforehand to modify such drinking behaviors

• If thoughts of drinking consume the mind while driving home from work, that is a clear danger sign. If so, try to fill the mind with positive thoughts, a *mantra word* or *meaningful phrase*, to get rid of the negativity. Keep on repeating *God Help Me* or your favorite one, and after certain practice, you may wonder what happened to the thoughts about the cold ones in the fridge!

• Don't allow drinking to be the first activity when reaching home. Wait for an hour for the first beer, two hours would be even better. If thirsty, go for a non-alcoholic drink, perhaps coffee or tea, water will be even better Use the *waiting time,* to have quality time with family or indulge in a hobby

• While on a vacation make rules to limit drinking, perhaps only allowing drinks at dinner. For Christmas Eve, consider drinking only in the evening and after returning home from church. For July 4th, keep tab on the beer while barbecuing. Consult a physician for other options to deal with high anxiety in social situations rather that drinking more

• Also each person has to be aware of the modulating factors that can reduce the risk of drinking too much, and employ them wisely with full acknowledgment. Since food in the stomach is a well-known deterrent to drinking, snacking with the drink or eating a full meal after moderate drinking are good strategies. It may not be easy, since the bliss from drinking may be stronger than the pleasure from even the best piece of steak! However, by employing the power of mind and practicing this strategy on a regular basis, it will slowly get easier

• Another modulating factor that can be used to reduce drinking is sleep. Always keep in mind, the more hours a person has between the first drink of the day and sleep time, the greater the drinking dangerous. In this regard, the morning drinker would be at the highest risk and late evening drinker of lesser risk of messing up the day

• Some drinkers are likely to move from beer to hard liquor, claiming they've lost the taste for the cold one or are hoping to get rid of the beer belly, taking comfort in the smaller amounts consumed! Unfortunately, this is a dangerous escalation of an unhealthy behavior with hardly any benefits at all. Interestingly, some hard-liquor-people will switch to beer in an effort to reduce their drinking, only find they are unable to quench the biological thirst of their brains. It was reported that the Senator of the Cold War Era Joseph McCarthy often switched to beer to detoxify himself. He still developed cirrhosis of the liver and died at age 48.

CHAPTER 21
IT'S JUST THE POT

With several U.S. States having already legalized marijuana use or approved its medical usage, the genie is already out of the bottle on a grand scale. Even President Barack Obama joined this discussion, saying in an interview with *The New Yorker* magazine. "As has been well documented, I smoked pot as a kid, and I view it as a bad habit and vice, not very different from cigarettes that I smoked as a young person up through a big chunk of my adult life. I don't think it is more dangerous than alcohol."

Pot vs Booze

The vast majority of Americans went a step further than the carefully-crafted words of President, saying alcohol was more harmful to a person's health than marijuana. A Pew survey showed that 69 percent of them believed so; only 15 percent indicated marijuana was worse. Nearly half of Americans said they tried it, 12 percent in the year prior to the survey. In parallel with the public opinion, the idea of legalizing marijuana gained momentum, 53 percent of people supporting it. This was in sharp contrast to the survey in 1969 when Gallup first asked the same question, it found that just 12 percent favored such legalization. These are the known facts about marijuana vs. alcohol:

- Drinking too much alcohol quickly can kill a person. "You can die binge-drinking. That isn't going to happen with marijuana," said Ruben Baler, a health scientist at the National Institute on Drug Abuse. "The impact of marijuana use is much subtler."
- Both excessive alcohol consumption and marijuana smoking can take a toll on the body and mind, their short-term effects are well-understood. However, less is known about the impact of long-

term usage of marijuana. According to Joe Brownstein, a contributing writer to *Live Science*, concerns about marijuana's impact has been raised about reproduction, certain cancers, worsening of mental diseases, and more definite bronchitis, coughing and chronic inflammation of the air passages. The death rate from alcohol has more clearly identified and according to Center for Disease Control, it has been linked to some 88,000 deaths per year, brought on by multitude of causes ranging from cirrhosis of liver to motor vehicle accidents

• Unlike the research of previous decades that focused more on the ill-effects of marijuana, the modern research is paying more attention to the medical benefits of this substance. Alcohol, too, in moderation, has been shown to have health benefits. According to National institute of alcohol abuse and alcoholism, moderate drinking can reduce stress and anxiety. Also, there is considerable body of evidence that lower levels of drinking decrease the risk of death from coronary artery disease

• Both alcohol and marijuana are recognized for harmful interactions with prescription medications, over-the-counter drugs and even some herbal products

Medical Marijuana

The earliest recorded marijuana use dates from the 3rd millennium BC. However, journal articles began to emerge only from the middle of 19th century, mostly documenting its benefits to treat "neuralgia, convulsive disorders, emaciation," among other things. From the early 20th century on, the legal trend was to constrain its use, stressing more on its ill effects. Still, until 1943 marijuana was part of the United States drug pharmacopeia, one common condition for which it prescribed was neuropathic pain. Interestingly in 1944, New York Mayor Fiorello LaGuardia commissioned research to be performed by the New York Academy of Science. Among their conclusions: they found marijuana did not lead to significant addiction in the medical sense of the word. They also did not find any evidence marijuana led to morphine, heroin or cocaine addiction.

Still, in 1970 marijuana entered the FDA schedule of category one of substances that have no accepted medical use and noted to have a high potential for abuse. Those who disagreed soon began with attempts to decriminalize it. In 1996 California legalized medical cannabis and this was followed by several other states. Recreational legalization began in 2012 with Colorado and Washington legalizing such usage for adults 21 years of age or older and the trend continued to other U.S states. Very recently, a bi-partisan group of U.S. representatives formed the first-ever "Congressional Cannabis Caucus" to work on legislation related to marijuana legalization and regulation!

Wynne Armand, M.D, wrote on the medical usage of marijuana in Harvard Health Publications August 21, 2016 and pointed out its appetite stimulant property in AIDS patients and for chemotherapy-related nausea and vomiting. The research is on the potential benefits in drug-resistant epilepsy, some psychiatric disorders like PTSD, for treatment of multiple sclerosis muscle spasticity and cancer-related pain not managed by other pain medication.

Do the physicians, the guardians of America's health, a group more conservative in their outlook than the general population smoke marijuana? According to the 2015 *Medscape Life Style* report a quarter of them tried it and about 3 percent did so in the past year. Elin Kondrad and Alfred Reid surveyed the Colorado Family Physicians' attitudes toward medical marijuana. Of the 520 family physicians who responded to the survey 19 percent thought that physicians should recommend it, 27 percent thought marijuana conferred significant physical benefits and 15 percent though it conferred significant mental health benefits. In a recent survey, when asked if they would approve the use of marijuana to help ease a woman's pain from breast cancer, 76% of the physicians said, yes!

Change of Mind

In 2013 Dr. Sanjay Gupta, CNN Chief Medical Correspondent revealed, "Why I changed my mind on weed" and said, we have been "systemically misled" on marijuana. The nationally well-respected surgeon went on to say, "Well, I am here to apologize. I apologize because I didn't look hard enough, until now. I didn't look far enough. I didn't review papers from smaller labs in other countries doing some remarkable research, and I was too dismissive of the loud chorus of legitimate patients whose symptoms improved on cannabis. Instead, I lumped them with the high-visibility malingerers, just looking to get high. I mistakenly believed the Drug Enforcement Agency listed marijuana as a schedule one substance because of sound scientific proof. Surely, they must have quality reasoning as to why marijuana is in the category of the most dangerous drugs that have—no accepted medicinal use and a high potential for abuse."

He went on to say, "We now know that while estimates vary, marijuana leads to dependence in around 9 to 10% of its adult users. By comparison, cocaine, a schedule two substance—with less abuse potential than schedule one drugs—hooks 20% of those who use it. Around 25% of heroin users become addicted. The worst is tobacco, where the number is closer to 30% of smokers—"

Commenting on the medical benefits he said, "Here is the problem. Most of these medications don't work very well for this kind of pain, and tolerance is a real problem. Most frightening to me is that someone dies in the United States every 19 minutes from a prescription drug overdose, mostly accidental. Every 19 minutes. It is a horrifying statistic. As much as I searched, I could not find a documented case of death from marijuana overdose."

Concerns

Why should there be any concerns about marijuana today, with its wider acceptance all over the world? The United Nations estimated that more than 3.8 percent of the world's population use marijuana and the National Institute on Drug Abuse's 2009 national survey showed more than 104 million Americans over the age of 12 had tried marijuana at least once, and almost 17 million used it in the month before the survey. In 2008, marijuana was reported in over 374,000 emergency department visits in the U.S., about 13 percent involving people between the ages of 12 and 17.

Another concern with marijuana, its potency has been increasing steadily with higher risk to the users. Joseph M. Pierre, M.D at David Geffen School of Medicine at UCLA, Los Angeles wrote in a recent issue of Current Psychiatry—Whereas the THC content of street marijuana was less than 1% in the 1970s and 4% in the 1990s, by 2012, analysis of cannabis samples seized by law enforcement agencies documented a rise in average THC to more than 12%. The author pointed out, "As the THC levels rise, the risk of psychosis, cognitive deficits, and structural brain changes increases."

The concerns with adult usage of marijuana are its association with unsatisfactory work, domestic problems and impaired coordination leading to traffic accidents. According to Drug Enforcement Administration, next to alcohol, marijuana was the second most frequently found substance in the bodies of drivers involved in fatal automobile accidents. Data revealed, people high on marijuana showed the same lack of coordination on standard drunk driver tests as did people with too much to drink. Also, nationwide 40 percent of adult males tested positive for it, when arrested for other crimes.

The concerns in young users is its higher risk of addiction and complications in them, in the form of memory and concentration problems, leading to poor academic performance. In one survey, 59 percent of marijuana-using students reported forgetting what a conversation was about before the conversation ended. A 1995 study of college students discovered that for 24 hours after their last use of the drug, the heavy marijuana users were unable to focus, sustain attention and organize data. On top of this, the Center on Addiction and Substance Abuse at Columbia University (CASA) found that 60 percent of youngsters who used marijuana before they turned 15, later went on to use other mind-altering drugs, including prescription medications.

With the rapid increase in public acceptance, it is highly likely marijuana will be legalized across the United States. How long will it take is anybody's guess! In the meantime, everyone should be educated to its harmful effects as well, more so the youngsters. Parents should not have a double standard, one for marijuana and another for hard drugs.

PART IV
DIAGNOSTIC
PROBLEMS

CHAPTER 22
DIAGNOSTIC LABEL

O n January 28, 2011, Demi Lovato, the singer and songwriter completed inpatient treatment at Timberline Knolls and returned home holding onto her psychiatric diagnosis. In her speech at the National Alliance on Mental Illness Annual National Convention, she said, "It's my mission to share this with the world and to let them know that there is life on the other side of those dark times that seem so hopeless and helpless. I want to show the world that there is life—surprising, wonderful and unexpected life after *diagnosis*."

Patty Duke

The award-winning actress wrote her autobiography, *Call Me Anna*, revealing a story of abuse and rebellion, courage and survival and finally leading to ultimate triumph. She also wrote about getting a diagnosis after going through years of professional upheavals, rocky relationships, suicidal behavior and hospitalization: "When I walked into (Dr. Harold) Arlen's office, I was very shaky. He said—Now, I don't want you to be frightened by what I'm about say to you. I suspected this before, but because it's such a delicate thing to pinpoint, and it's something you really don't want to be wrong about, I wanted to be as sure as I could. I think you are manic-depressive." Duke disclosed in the book the instant relief she received, "From that moment on, I wasn't frightened at all. It was such a relief, almost like a miracle, really, for someone to give what I'd gone through a name and treatment, and I am ever in Dr. Arlen's debt for having the skill and insight to *diagnose* me."

The verdict delivered by the benevolent healer can be simple and straightforward, capable of soothing the anxious beholder, or complex and cumbersome, bruising the terrified onlooker. The revelation can bring in cheers of joy—pregnant for the first time, or spread out the dark shadows of catastrophic gloom—terminal cancer.

Self-Diagnosis

This day and age, most people approaching a physician will have some inkling what is wrong with them. This is brought on by their good education, exposure to widespread media coverage and self-learning through the internet. Medical experts encourage this consumer approach, patient forming a team with the physician in search for their diagnosis and actively get involved in their treatment.

Many patients succeed in suspecting even a major illness by doing their homework diligently, thus making the doc's job easier. In a neurology text book, there is a story of a grandmother in a Huntington's disease family who correctly predicted which children would develop it, based on her observation of their *clumsy* behavior. With this autosomal-dominant neurological disease, half the children would be afflicted by it in adulthood.

For some patients, the family health diagnosis would be the driving force behind their search for a diagnosis and seeking help—my brother died of heart attack; he was under the age of 55; I definitely should see a cardiologist—my mother died of breast cancer and now my sister has been diagnosed with ovarian cancer; I should get the genetic testing for the mutations in *BRCA1* and *BRCA2*—my mother has bipolar disorder; I should check if my major depression at any risk of turning to the same.

Some patients would have their diagnosis by a name, while seeking help—I have flu, the cough not going away—I believe it is poison ivy, the itching drives me crazy—I am sure my daughter has chickenpox, it is in their school or I have PTSD, I was sexually assaulted—my son has ADHD, he cannot sit still—I cannot stand my husband coming home with dirty shoes, may be it is OCD.

Mind problems are easily self-identifiable most of the time, the concern will be in downplaying their significance. Stress and anxiety can be continuously irritating and obvious to those who are afflicted, however, others like greed and arrogance may not come out of hiding every day, needing more introspection and insight to recognize them as significant. Some people with anger problem and impulsivity would be deeply puzzled when the phone call came from the Family Services or the cops showed up at the front door with arrest warrant.

Missteps

The strategy of creating own diagnosis, if carefully carried out, can pay huge dividends. However, if attention not paid to the details and seeking professional help delayed, there can be serious consequences. Every illness has its unique set of complications—flu may have become aspiration pneumonia—food poisoning leading to dehydration—foot infection turning into septicemia, or a God-abiding person has suicidal depression—a young mother with normal post-partum blues, has become paranoid.

A family with bipolar illness reported their 18-year-old daughter had a severe paranoid reaction after ingesting cocaine *once,* and took a *full week* to recover. With further search, they found out that the grandfather had molested her when she was young. The action-oriented family wanted to attack both problems at the same time, having her attend substance abuse classes, while getting psychotherapy for the sexual abuse!

Both approaches would have failed. With a family history of bipolar disorder, the daughter was at an age to manifest the same illness. Definitely, she had not yet had a manic or depressive episode, however, an unusual reaction of paranoia that began with a one-time cocaine ingestion and required a week to recover may be was the clue to her vulnerability to develop it later. With this situation, the prime focus of management has to be prevention of bipolar disorder, educating the teenager on the dangers of using illicit drugs and even prescription drugs with psychostimulant property. In addition, she should practice good sleep hygiene and not dismiss even mild mood swings as insignificant or as simply a part of normal day-to-day living.

Those who self-diagnose their health problems should not overestimate their ability and keep in mind that the missteps do occur even for the well-qualified physicians. David Troxel, MD, medical director of The Doctors Company and colleagues analyzed 464 claims against the 2100 hospitalists the company insures that closed from 2007 to 2014 and released the findings at the Society of Hospital Medicine 2016 Annual Meeting. They found that 36% of the claims were related to diagnoses, including missed, late, or incorrect ones.

Chicken or Egg?

Missteps do happen, when caught up in the causality dilemma that commonly stated as, "Which came first, the chicken or the egg?" For a person who appeared sad after losing the job, the search should look for any depressive symptoms before getting fired, to find out if the job loss caused by lack of productivity and frequently sick calls. Did the breakup in marriage cause the miserable feeling or the depressed mood already there led to the erosion in the quality of relationship?

With better genetic knowledge today and knowing the brain is more in control than we used to believe, the clinical disorders and mind problems are more likely to be the cause rather than the consequence of a life adversity. In many situations, it can be both. It is highly important to reach the right conclusions, since wrong ones can lead to taking improper strategies to solve them. If depression caused the job loss, such a person should receive professional treatment before venturing to another job. If the marriage breakup was due to an emotional problem, the primary focus should be management of that problem, rather than marriage counseling. Nobody is immune to these missteps, even the well-educated and smart people can succumb to it.

Story of a Physician

A physician, who also happened to be a patient, revealed her mental anguish. "-- I was about to start a residency program at a prestigious institution. It seemed as if my hard work had paid off and my dreams were realized. However, six weeks into my residency, I was in trouble. I was repeatedly unable to complete my work in a timely fashion. I had trouble concentrating on even the simplest of tasks, I noted with dismay that I was often unable to recall basic facts I had read—I remained slow, inefficient, disorganized. It seemed as if my mind was paralyzed.

Slowly I began to wonder if I was contracting some sort of dementia.

I was diagnosed with depression. Curiously, the diagnosis did not come as much of a relief. My condition proved to be a very isolating experience, and the isolation only intensified the disease and its accompanying shame and loneliness—However, the diagnosis did allow me to finally receive proper treatment with medication and psychotherapy." Like this physician who wondered if she contracting some sort of dementia, it was not unusual for some people with OCD to worry if they were going crazy or someone with panic attacks worry of dying from heart attack. Fortunately for this physician, she received the necessary help at Physician Health Services (PHS) in Massachusetts.

Professional Diagnosis

The ancient people afflicted with ailments and frailties, not fully satisfied with the ripostes from their gods, approached the shamans and pagan priests to find out the wrongness. Many received comfort and relief by subjecting themselves to mystifying rituals and bewildering magic. Millenniums changed hands and the healer's sacred role moved through Greece, Egypt, Rome, India and China, and finally the modern doctor arrived on the scene, leaving behind the primitive practices of yesterdays. Today, millions in distress visit their physicians to get a proper diagnosis based on solid scientific principles and this has become an integral part of modern medicine.

To avoid diagnostic mistakes, the physicians employ several time-honored tools, the most important element of them all is the health history. As a detective searching for clues, the physician will pay attention to the person behind the story, to reliability of history, amount of distress displayed and the individual's expectations. While listening to the words, the physician' mind would be entertaining various diagnostic possibilities, narrowing them down to at least a provisional diagnosis by end of the session. Experienced clinicians trust a reliable history the most in their search for diagnosis, employing physical examination, lab tests and procedures to confirm it.

Each physician has his or her own unique style in eliciting the clinical history, no two docs will be alike in this endeavor. However, the general format will consist of *Chief Complaint*, to learn what brought the patient for consultation, *History of Present Illness* (HPI) that will expand the chief complaint to understand the underlying problem(s) better, *Past History* to find out if any link between current illness and the clinical events happened before, *Family Health History* to assess any genetic/family component to the patient's illness and *Personal/Social History* to elicit any relevant such data that can influence not only the diagnosis, but the prognosis and treatment as well.

Diagnosis becomes a major part of the evaluation, wrapping up all the relevant pieces of pain and discomfort into clean packages, with its ability to provide instant relief and peace of mind to many people, however, also has the capability to cause distress and even shock some others. Many would be rewarded with the miracles of modern medicine, even though their health conditions were cumbersome and complicated.

There would be many clinical situations in which the full diagnosis may not forthcoming, if so, the physician would make provisional diagnosis, may even entertain more than one diagnosis, ruling out the irrelevant ones by collecting more relevant data. With the complexity of human body, many patients, especially the elderly would have multiple diagnoses brought on by their physical examination, lab investigations and radiological tests. The complex human mind too often needs detailed conclusions, since unable to place all the relevant problems in one neatly-knitted basket.

Arriving at a medical diagnosis is based on several well-proven scientific principles. However, making a mental health diagnosis becomes more challenging, with less verified theories on its side, and also because the symptoms can greatly be influenced by the patient's personality, education, culture and religious beliefs. With less science on his side, Dr. Arlen was very careful how he conveyed Duke her diagnosis of manic- depressive illness.

Implications

Every diagnosis has its own consequences, sometimes only resulting in minor inconveniences, however, has the ability to cause profound sadness, even shock the person beyond belief. Psychiatric diagnosis can have a totally different set of implications, partially brought on by the prevailing social stigma. Will I lose my job with the alcoholic diagnosis? Will my cannabis dependence make it hard to get back the custody of my little one? Will my bipolar diagnosis prevent me adopting a child from Mexico? Will my relatives use my diagnosis to declare me mentally incompetent and grab my money? Will my children lock me up claiming I was paranoid? Since these fears can be realistic and have the potential to cause roadblocks on the way, it is not unusual at all, for some patients hide certain problems or try to mislead the provider.

Mind problems are unique in that they do not have to carry the burden of social stigma in front of others. For most in the public, the admission of stress in marriage or burnout from a job is well-understandable, without labeling them as weaknesses of the mind. Getting anxious before job interview or nervous during wedding ceremony, well, they are normal too! Arrogant behavior or anger problems will raise concerns, however, they are easily understandable. The downfall of mind problem lie in ignoring them or downplaying their significance and suffering the consequences.

CHAPTER 23
DIAGNOSTIC
CHALLENGES

I t is not unusual for medical students and interns during their training to get fascinated by an exotic diagnosis that they encountered for the first time. Even though they may come across such one, only once or twice in their life time, still the interesting diagnosis dwell in their brains more firmly and influence them to think less of common diagnoses. Seeing this pitfall in their training, Dr. Theodore Woodward, Professor at the School of Medicine, University of Maryland told them on the importance of paying attention to the more commonplace diagnoses than the exotic ones. To emphasize the point, he coined the adage, "When you hear hoof beats, think of horses not zebras."

Zebras may not be found in Maryland, however, in this day and age of rapid travel, it is not unusual for an infection contracted in Nairobi or Mogadishu to emerge out as a disease in New York or Chicago. A disease prevalent in an Asian country such as tuberculosis or malaria may show up in Boston or St Louis as a tuberculoma or encephalitis, increasing the risk of misdiagnosis. Rarely an entirely novel disorder or an old one in a new uniform with a strange name make their appearance puzzling the U.S. doctors. It can be *Ianti* from Philippines or *Saladera* from the Peruvian Amazon or *Latah* from Malaysia or *Ainu* from Japan.

With the intimate relationship between the body and mind, it is not unusual for some well- recognized medical disorders initially present with psychological symptoms. An undetected hypothyroidism or Addison's disease or a left frontal meningioma of the brain or even pancreatic cancer can come out of nowhere, spreading depressive gloom before heralding the somatic symptoms. Adrenal tumor pheochromocytoma is known to pump out hormones more that needed, precipitating panic attacks. In a family afflicted with hereditary neurological illness Huntington's disease, some members may exhibit severe anxiety and memory problems before showing its characteristic *dancing* movements of hand and feet.

Misdiagnosis

Mark Graber, founder and president of the Society to Improve Diagnosis in Medicine warned, "You have a good chance of being misdiagnosed if you have a really rare disease or a really common disease which presents non-specifically or in some atypical fashion." A 1999 Institute of Medicine report was an eye-opener for many and sent shockwaves across the medical community—up to 98,000 people die each year in U.S. due to hospital mistakes! A 2013 study published in the *Journal of Patient Safety* projected that the medical errors now accounting for 210,000 to 440,000 deaths annually. Seniors are at higher risk of suffering medical injuries when receiving care. A study of more than 12,500 Medicare patients with an average age of 76 found that nearly one in five suffered from medical injuries when receiving care. For those with disabilities, the risk rose 27 percent for each chronic medical condition a person had. There are multiple causes for this ongoing tragedy, one of the major ones is the missed diagnosis.

This seemingly unforgivable tragedy can occur in any clinical setting, even in the high-rated hospitals and in the nation's best teaching facilities and patient can belong to any specialty, psychiatric patients having their share. According to the journal *BMJ Quality & Safety*, each year in the U.S, approximately 12 million adults who seek outpatient medical care are misdiagnosed. This did not include the care provided in other medical settings including inpatient care, also excluded the children. The report raised the frightening possibility, most people would suffer from at least one wrong or delayed medical diagnosis during their lifetime! The researchers pointed out that in half of those cases, the misdiagnosis had the potential to result in severe harm. CBS News chief medical correspondent Dr. Jon LaPook said, "It represents about 5 percent of the outpatient encounters. Getting 95 percent right might be good on a school history test, but it's not good enough for medicine especially when lives are at stake.

Atpicality

Zebras may be rare, horses more common, however, there will be hot-blooded wild horses make their entrance confusing everyone. These are the atypical diagnoses, the physicians encounter from time to time, posing diagnostic challenges. Multiple factors come into play in making an illness atypical and age is one of them.

It is well-known, the elderly with frail bodies are less likely to exhibit fever and leukocytosis with infection, and pain and discomfort with acute abdomen. The symptoms of heart attack and heart failure can be vague in this patient population and clinical depression may manifest in them with impaired memory, rather than sadness. The senior citizens are also at the disadvantage of having multiple medical conditions, thereby needing several medications and increasing the risk of atypical presentations.

At the other end of age-spectrum, the adolescents can exhibit with atypical symptoms, confusing their diagnosis. National Institute of Mental Health reported that these youngsters when manic were more likely to be irritable and prone to destructive outbursts, and when depressed there may be many physical complaints such as headaches, stomachaches or tiredness, poor performance in school, irritability, social isolation, and extreme sensitivity to rejection or failure. The unrecognized stress brought on by getting bullied at school can come out in youngsters as a behavior problem at home.

Another diagnostic error related to age occurs by associating a disorder or illness with certain age group. Teenagers with an early onset bipolar disorder can easily get misdiagnosed with ADHD due similarities in their symptoms, and also due to increased awareness of ADHD. Parkinsonism is less likely to be considered as a diagnosis, when a 30 year old develops shaky hands. Actor Michael J. Fox was at that age when he received such diagnosis. Alzheimer's is more likely to be considered as a possible diagnosis, when elderly develop memory problems, however, Pat Summitt who holds the record for the most all-time wins for a coach in NCAA basketball history of either a men's or women's team in any division and recipient of the Presidential Medal of Freedom was in her 50s when diagnosed with it. ALS, later named Lou Gehrig disease typically manifests between the ages 40 and 70; however, he retired from major league baseball at age 36 after receiving his diagnosis. With FDR, his age of onset of paralysis from waist down at age 39 caused a different kind of confusion. He was given the diagnosis of poliomyelitis, a common illness then, even though it was recognized as infantile paralysis. The Polio diagnosis was later questioned and experts came up with the opinion that the President suffered from Guillain–Barré syndrome.

Gender is another major factor in causing atypicality, a good example is of the women suffering heart attack more likely to have unusual fatigue, sleep disturbance and shortness of breath and many of them do not develop typical chest pain, like the men. Even if there was pain, a 2003 NIH study reported that it was less likely to radiate to left arm, and more to the other body parts. These types of atypical presentations, coupled with the perception that the women not likely to have heart attacks have led to higher mortality for them. Across all age groups, the women fared badly, 42 percent of them died within one year of the attack, while that percentage for men was 24. Another concern, the younger women are even more likely to be ignored while having a heart attack. According to Women's Heart Foundation 435,000 American women have heart attacks annually and out of that 35,000 under 55, and they have even much higher death rates than other women.

Another misconception is considering the heart attack as a disease of senior citizens; however, as many as 4 to 10 percent of this heart disease occur in men before the age of 45. Talk-show host Larry King lost his father to a heart attack at age 43 and he himself suffered one at age 53. The general tendency to associate an illness with a certain population can also be misleading. Yes, smokers are more likely to develop lung cancer; however, about 10–15 percent of this cancer occur in those who never smoked. Only women develop breast cancer? No! Men account for about one percent of this cancer. Associating an illness with certain patient population has its distinct advantages, but also has significant limitations.

Addictive Part

From time immemorial, the mankind has been fascinated with alcohol and drugs for varied reasons. Many used alcohol on a regular basis—just to feel good- the taste of it—simply to relax and so on, with no much concern if the consumption was in moderation. However, if the *devil* got out of control, it was branded as lack of will, absence of motivation, moral failure, even sin and evil. The modern world found out that quit drinking took more than good intentions and will power, and many viewed addiction as a complex disease brought on by genetics and environment, may be by messing up the brain's reward circuit, flooding it with the chemical messenger dopamine. However, the transient pleasures brought on by the chemical, also provided instant relief of distressing symptoms, perpetuating the addiction.

There is less talk today about primary versus secondary addiction, since the lines separating them are highly blurred. There is plenty of evidence, the vast majority of addicted people having underlying mental disorders, the chemical substance is used to relieve the emotional distress. If subclinical disorders and significant mind problems are taken into account, it is very much possible everyone has a secondary addiction!

The addiction poses unique diagnostic challenges, even if the chemical offender is identified. Each substance has distinctly different effect on the brain and mind, distorting the presentations of clinical depressions and anxiety disorders and covering up the subclinical disorders and significant mind problems. Even the reliable diagnostic criteria will take a backseat to the smell of alcohol or bizarre behavior of drug intoxication.

Frequent Flyer

Johnson had the reputation of being a frequent flyer with multiple admissions to the psychiatric unit. There was a clear pattern precipitating them—alcohol intoxication, getting into altercations, followed by suicidal threats to avoid going to jail. Once admitted, he wandered inside the ward like a raging bull, breaking rules, enraging the staff, upsetting other patients and precipitating fights. Obnoxious and hostile, yelling and screaming, his outbursts were usually about not being able to smoke. Within a day or two, he either signed himself out or got discharged to the relief of staff and other patients. His diagnoses were always the same—alcohol intoxication, alcohol dependence and antisocial personality disorder. However, a big surprise happened during his last admission.

This occurred on a summer day in 2003. Surprisingly, he was not inebriated and appeared unusually quiet. He did not come to the nurse's station as usual demanding more food, nor was he upset about the smoking rules. He spent long hours in bed and hardly spoke. The staff had to wake him up for each meal that he hardly ate. Having seen all telltale signs of clinical depression, the physician wondered if his previous presentations of obnoxiousness and hostility could have been due to hypomania, and not completely from alcohol intoxication or a personality disorder. Johnson stayed in the hospital longer this time and was treated with an antidepressant and mood stabilizer. His mood began to improve. His diagnosis was changed to bipolar disorder and alcohol dependence. He received social security benefits with the new diagnosis and agreed to stay in a boarding home under supervision.

Expert Advice

Institute of Medicine committee recommended several changes to correct the alarming trend of wrong diagnosis:

- More training (in medical school and continuing education) in making diagnoses
- Increased collaboration among pathologists, radiologists, other diagnosticians, and health care professions to improve the diagnostic process
- Increased monitoring of how health care facilities are diagnosing patients. Federal agencies and employers should encourage the reporting of diagnostic errors to help others learn how to avoid them
- Encouraging patients to be involved in their care and share concerns about diagnostic errors.
- Ensuring patients have access to electronic health records, diagnostic testing results, etc. so they can review for accuracy

The most critical element in managing this national tragedy is the active involvement of patient through every step of their care. Dr. Peter Pronovost, Director of the Armstrong Institute for Patient Safety and

Quality at Johns Hopkins emphasized, "We need to encourage patients to speak up and ensure that when they do speak up, it's well received." The National Patient Safety Foundation and the Society to Improve Diagnosis in Medicine came up with a check list for patients:

- Tell your story well; when symptoms started, what makes symptoms better or worse, etc.
- Remember what treatments you've tried in the past and how the illness has progressed over time
- Keep records of test results, medications, and hospital admissions
- Learn about your illness, tests or procedures you're having done, and/or medications you're taking
- Take charge of managing your health, and be sure each doctor you're seeing is aware of other doctors' visits, medications you're taking, test results, treatments, etc.
- Be actively involved in your health care decisions
- Know your tests results, including what the results mean
- Ask questions, including whether there could be other reasons or causes for your illness

Mental Health

The diagnostic challenges in the mental health field are brought on by the lack of objective data and not having much support from physical findings, lab investigations and procedures. The clinical history and mental status examination become the supreme tools in arriving at a diagnosis. Since they are the bedrock of correct diagnosis, the patient reliability in providing history becomes even more important in this setting. Some patients would be notoriously unreliable and unable to provide meaningful history. There would be others, who purposefully cover up the truth or even outright lie for a certain secondary gain, may be to receive disability or get a controlled medication.

Even with the well-reliable patients, many psychiatrists would consider having a responsible family member coming with the patient extremely useful, at least for the initial evaluation. Such second-hand information can help the provider to add to the history obtained from the patient and chisel out if any unnecessary data. Also important for the patient to bring with them a list of medications they are currently taking, as well as any relevant records from other sources. These commonsense steps can tremendously reduce the risk of receiving a misdiagnosis.

In the midst of typical and atypical disorders, the good health providers would not ignore the significant mind problems that could cause harm by themselves, and also due to unhealthy coping method adopted by their patients. Having kept at the lower end of the fulcrum without proper dressing, they may miss the glamor and glitter of classical clinical disorders. However, those providers who venture into this exciting arena would be richly rewarded by increased patient satisfaction.

CHAPTER 24
'NAM TO 'BINE

The psychoanalysis-tainted quandary faced by psychiatric experts in dealing with the concept of *stress* was partially solved by bringing *Post-Traumatic Stress Disorder* into the diagnostic fold after 'Nam, however, unfortunately continued even after that, and on an April day in 1999 'Bine became a major symbol of it, as two teenagers Dylan Klebold and Eric Harris unleashed terror in Columbine High School in Colorado.

ABC Interview

Dylan's mother told television journalist Diane Sawyer that before the attack, she considered herself a parent who would have known something was wrong. "I think we like to believe that our love and our understanding is protective, and that 'if anything were wrong with my kids, I would know,' but I didn't know... If I had recognized that Dylan was experiencing some real mental distress, he would not have been there. He would have gotten help."

The distressed mother wrote in *O magazine* that her son had a fun childhood. "I taught him how to protect himself from a host of dangers: lightning, snake bites, head injuries, skin cancer, smoking, drinking, sexually transmitted diseases, drug addiction, reckless driving, even carbon monoxide poisoning. It never occurred to me that the gravest danger to him and, as it turned out to so many others, might come from within."

Profile

Polly Palumbo wrote an article in *Psychology Today* titled, "Profile of a Rampage Killer: What do we know about the typical school shooter?" It dealt with a study by the Department of Education that teamed up with U.S. Secret Service, examining the 41 school shooters in the U.S. between 1974 and 2000. Their conclusion: There was no accurate or useful profile of who would carry out the school attacks. The data revealed:

- They ranged in age and ethnicity, and almost all of them were male
- Most came from two-parent families (63%); only 20% from one-parent households
- Most did well in school with 41% getting As and Bs. Some had taken AP courses and were on the honor roll. Only 5% were failing. None showed any pre-attack slip in grades
- Almost half of them were considered to be part of the mainstream crowd at school. Only 27% belonged to a fringe group or hung with students considered fringe by the mainstream. Only 34% were loners
- Almost two-thirds never or rarely got into trouble at school. Few had either been suspended (27%) or expelled (10%)
- Most (71%) felt they'd been bullied, persecuted, or harmed by other people right before the attack. Some had been bullied from early childhood, some not at all
- Most had expressed the feelings of suicide (78%) and depression (61%) though only a third of them received mental health evaluation and a fifth diagnosed with a mental disorder. Only less than a quarter had a known history of drug or alcohol abuse
- Most had trouble coping with significant loss or failures in their young lives before the attack (98%)
- Most were into violent media—movies, video games, books, etc. (59%). More than a third of them wrote violent poems, essays, or stories; 15% played violent video games
- Most had no history of violence or criminal behavior. Only a third had acted violent towards another student in the past and a quarter had been arrested

• Most (93%) didn't snap or carry out attacks on an impulse or whim but planned the attacks, some for years in advance. Typically other people knew about the plan, sometimes even helped to plan or prepare. In almost all the cases (93%) the young man did something that deeply concerned someone prior to the attack. In almost three-quarters, at least three people were very worried

The U.S. Secret Service urged adults to look for the following:

• What has this child said?
• Do they have grievances?
• What do their friends know?
• Do they have access to weapons?
• Are they depressed or despondent?

Identifying a future school killer may be a million times worse than searching for a tiny, weeny needle in a gigantic haystack. Did it mean we need to give up this search and put up with it as inevitable, knowing very well it would happen again? Are we to simply cry out foul each time a horrific incident happened, the tough gun lobby defending the citizens' right to bear arms, the social experts getting suspicious of parental skills in bringing up their *sons*, and the politicians blaming each other for not providing enough funds for mental health?

Let us take another look at the study by the Department of Education that concluded there was no accurate or useful profile of who would carry out school attacks. In spite of this highly pessimistic conclusion, certain numbers stood out as highly significant:

• 71% felt they'd been *bullied, persecuted, or harmed* by other people right before attack
• 78% felt *suicidal* and 61% *depressed*
• 98% had trouble coping with *significant loss or failures* in their young lives
• 59% were into *violent media*—movies, video games, books, etc.
• 93% didn't snap or carry out attacks on an impulse or whim but *planned attacks*, some for years in advance. Typically *other people knew about the plan*, sometimes even helping to plan or prepare
• In 93% of cases the young man did something that deeply concerned someone prior to the attack. In almost three-quarters, *at*

least three people were very worried.

Prevention

How can we prevent these atrocious acts of carnage committed in the sanctuary of our nation's schools? I strongly believe there is hope, if the richest nation in the world willing to make a firm commitment. Here, I am putting forward a cost-effective national plan, a two-pronged strategy to be implemented together, stressing on prevention.

The first step is educational—educating the youngsters, parents, and teachers to make them more aware of:

- *Depression* and warning signs of *suicide*
- *Bullying* and its psychological effects
- *Grief* and dealing with a loss
- Danger signs of *violent talk* and preoccupation with *violent media*
- Dangers over the youngsters having access to *firearms*

The second step is for parents answering a Questionnaire at the beginning of each semester with active involvement of their child.

- Have your child appear *depressed?*
- Have your child talk about *suicide?*
- Have your child suffer any *significant loss?*
- Have your child access to *firearms?*
- Have your child *bullied?*
- Have your child fascinated with *violent media?*
- Have your child say anything inappropriate in reference to *violence?*

Each school should collect this data, analyze it in meaningful ways and identify those undergoing psychological turmoil and in need of intervention. Depending on the risks, monitoring and interventions have to be on-going, and no problem counted too small or trivial, or dismissed as subclinical or a mind problem. It is important for the parents and guardians to be involved in every facet of it. The children of America deserve this. Even those children who may not otherwise receive psychological help can benefit from it. Who knows—it may even reduce truancy, school dropout rates, crimes, and incarcerations! In all likelihood, it can reduce the risk of future school shootings as well.

Diagnosis

What was the psychiatric diagnosis of the Columbine boys who carried out the massacre that sent shockwaves across the nation? What about the other youngsters who took innocent lives inside their schools across the country? The *Psychology Today* article pointed out that very few had a mental health evaluation and even fewer received a psychiatric diagnosis. The reason was simple—they did not have any significant mental disorders that stood out in public display.

Everyone would agree that Dylan and Eric were mentally disturbed. Who else would carry out such a heinous act? Was that all there to it? Were they insane? The public wanted to know. Maybe they were insane in the public eye, but not in a clinical sense. Is that all to it? Can the guardians of mental health and creators of diagnostic manuals provide the answers?

To avoid the embarrassment of future Columbines, the psychiatric establishment has to come forward boldly, as they did in 1980 in case of PTSD, and accept that even the common mind problems have the power to make human life unhappy and miserable, and result in devastating events. Including them in the Diagnostic Manual in a more clinically meaningful way as significant problems, not necessarily as mental disorders would be a step in the right direction, encouraging health providers to look for, identify, and manage them appropriately. In doing so, any *Mind Problem* with any of the following characteristics should be taken seriously:

- If it lasted a week or more or kept on repeating
- If it affected sleep or appetite
- If it raised personal, health, social, or legal concerns
- If it forced the person to adopt wrong coping methods
- If it emerged in a family already afflicted with mental disorders

The question of whether the Columbine boys have a psychiatric diagnosis still needs an answer. The cause and effect reasoning goes this way—two school kids killed 13 innocent people and injured 24 others. This was much different than antisocial behavior. Definitely, they were mentally deranged. No doubt about it. However, they did not have even a mental disorder. Then what? In all probability, what they had was a cluster of *Mind Problems*:

- A little bit of sadness and hopelessness
- A little bit of stress and feeling miserable
- A little bit of narcissistic injury and rage
- A little bit of suspiciousness and victimization
- A little bit of humiliation and desire for revenge
- A little bit of eccentricity and borderline tendency

Each one of them by itself was not powerful enough to cause much havoc. However, in a certain combination, along with access to *firearms*, they became extremely dangerous, capable of shooting up a mushroom cloud of shock and terror across the nation. The fallout continues even today.

OTHER
ANAPHORA LITERARY
PRESS TITLES

PLJ: Interviews with Gene
Ambaum and Corban Addison:
VII:3, Fall 2015
Editor: Anna Faktorovich

Architecture of Being
By: Bruce Colbert

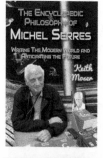

*The Encyclopedic Philosophy of
Michel Serres*
By: Keith Moser

Forever Gentleman
By: Roland Colton

Janet Yellen
By: Marie Bussing-Burks

*Diseases, Disorders, and Diagno-
ses of Historical Individuals*
By: William J. Maloney

Armageddon at Maidan
By: Vasyl Baziv

Vovochka
By: Alexander J. Motyl